Schweser Weekly Class Workbook
2017 Level I CFA®

Volume 1

SCHWESER WEEKLY CLASS WORKBOOK: 2017 LEVEL I CFA®,
VOLUME 1
©2016 Kaplan, Inc. All rights reserved.

Published in September 2016 by Kaplan Schweser.
Printed in the United States of America.

ISBN: 978-1-4754-4205-2

Contents

Study Session 2

Quantitative Methods: Basic Concepts

Quantitative Methods

Quantitative Methods: Basic Concepts

6. The Time Value of Money

KAPLAN UNIVERSITY SCHOOL OF PROFESSIONAL AND CONTINUING EDUCATION | SCHWESER

Quantitative Methods

Study Session 2
Quantitative Methods: Basic Concepts

6. The Time Value of Money
7. Discounted Cash Flow Applications
8. Statistical Concepts and Market Returns
9. Probability Concepts

KAPLAN UNIVERSITY SCHOOL OF PROFESSIONAL AND CONTINUING EDUCATION | SCHWESER

The Time Value of Money

LOS 6.c Calculate/Interpret
CFAI p. 311, Schweser p. 57

$100,000 CD has a stated annual rate of 3.6%.

1. What is the effective annual yield (EAY) if compounding is **quarterly**?

   Quarterly effective rate = 3.6% / 4 = 0.9%
   EAY = $(1.009)^4 - 1 = 3.649\%$

2. What is the EAY if compounding is **monthly**?

   Monthly effective rate = 3.6/12 = 0.3%
   EAY = $(1.003)^{12} - 1 = 3.66\%$

© Kaplan, Inc.

3 - 2

The Time Value of Money

LOS 6.b Explain
CFAI p. 303, Schweser p. 56

Components of Interest Rates

Required nominal interest rate on a security =

real risk-free rate ⎤ Nominal risk-free
+ expected inflation ⎦ rate

+ default risk premium ⎤
+ liquidity risk premium ⎬ Risk premium
+ maturity risk premium ⎦

© Kaplan, Inc.

2

LOS 6.c Calculate/Interpret
CFAI p. 311, Schweser p. 57 | **The Time Value of Money**

Effective Annual Rate BAII+

Now get EFF back on the screen by either:

[→] [→] [→] or [←]

EFF = [→] [CPT] = 3.6489%

© Kaplan, Inc.

5

LOS 6.c Calculate/Interpret
CFAI p. 311, Schweser p. 57 | **The Time Value of Money**

Stated Annual Rate BAII+

Stated annual rate with monthly compounding

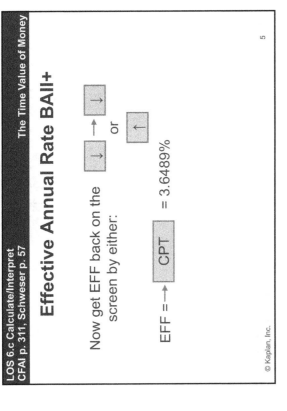

[2nd] → [2]   Access interest conversion

[2nd] → [CE/C]   Delete previously stored data

NOM =   Leave blank [↓]

EFF = [4.2] → [ENTER] [↓]

C/Y = # Compounding periods   [12] → [ENTER]

© Kaplan, Inc.

7

LOS 6.c Calculate/Interpret
CFAI p. 311, Schweser p. 57 | **The Time Value of Money**

Effective Annual Rate BAII+

Calculating effective quarterly rate

[2nd] → [2]   Access interest conversion

[2nd] → [CE/C]   Delete previously stored data

NOM = [3.6] → [ENTER] [↓]

EFF =   Leave blank [↓]

C/Y = # Compounding periods   [4] → [ENTER]

© Kaplan, Inc.

4

LOS 6.c Calculate/Interpret
CFAI p. 311, Schweser p. 57 | **The Time Value of Money**

A CD has an effective annual yield of 4.2%.

1. What is its stated annual rate if compounding is **quarterly?**

   Quarterly effective rate = $1.042^{1/4} - 1 = 1.034\%$

   Stated annual rate = $1.034\% \times 4 = 4.136\%$

2. What is the stated annual rate if compounding is **monthly?**

   Monthly effective rate = $1.042^{1/12} - 1 = 0.3434\%$

   Stated annual rate = $12 \times 0.3434 = 4.121\%$

© Kaplan, Inc.

6-2

Stated Annual Rate BAII+

Now get NOM back on the
screen by either:

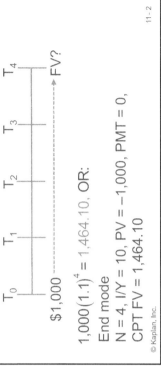

$NOM = \rightarrow \boxed{CPT} = 4.121\%$

© Kaplan, Inc.

8

Computing Periodic Payments BAII+

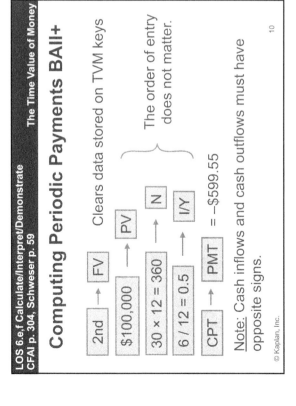

$\boxed{2nd} \rightarrow \boxed{FV}$ Clears data stored on TVM keys

$\boxed{\$100,000} \rightarrow \boxed{PV}$

$\boxed{30 \times 12 = 360} \rightarrow \boxed{N}$ The order of entry
does not matter.

$\boxed{6/12 = 0.5} \rightarrow \boxed{I/Y}$

$\boxed{CPT} \rightarrow \boxed{PMT} = -\$599.55$

Note: Cash inflows and cash outflows must have
opposite signs.

© Kaplan, Inc.

10

Computing Periodic Payments

What is the monthly payment on a $100,000,
30-year home loan with a stated rate of 6%?

T_0 T_1 T_2 T_{359} T_{360}

$100,000   PMT?   PMT?   PMT?   PMT?

END mode
N = 360, I/Y = 6/12 = 0.5, PV = 100,000, FV = 0,
CPT PMT = −599.55

© Kaplan, Inc.

9

Compounding and Future Value

What is the future value of $1,000 invested for four
years at 10% with annual compounding?

T_0 T_1 T_2 T_3 T_4

$1,000 -------------------- FV?

$1,000(1.1)^4 = 1,464.10$, OR:
End mode
N = 4, I/Y = 10, PV = −1,000, PMT = 0,
CPT FV = 1,464.10

© Kaplan, Inc.

11 - 2

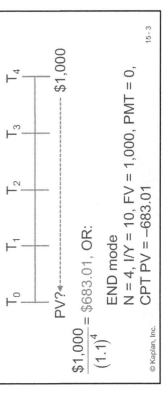

LOS 6.e,f Calculate/Interpret/Demonstrate The Time Value of Money
CFAI p. 304, Schweser p. 59

Future Value of a Single Cash Flow

What is the future value of $1,000 invested for four years at 10% with quarterly compounding?

T_0 T_1 T_2 ... T_{15} T_{16}

$1,000$ -------→ ?

$1,000(1.025)^{16} = 1,484.51$, OR:

END mode
N = 16, I/Y = 2.5, PV = –1,000, PMT = 0,
CPT FV = 1,484.51

© Kaplan, Inc.

13- 3

LOS 6.e,f Calculate/Interpret/Demonstrate The Time Value of Money
CFAI p. 304, Schweser p. 59

Present Value of a Single Sum

What is the present value of $1,000 to be received in four years when the interest rate is 10%

T_0 T_1 T_2 T_3 T_4

PV? -------→ $1,000

$$\frac{\$1,000}{(1.1)^4} = \$683.01, \text{ OR:}$$

END mode
N = 4, I/Y = 10, FV = 1,000, PMT = 0,
CPT PV = –683.01

© Kaplan, Inc.

15- 3

LOS 6.e,f Calculate/Interpret/Demonstrate The Time Value of Money
CFAI p. 304, Schweser p. 59

FV of Single Cash Flow BAII+

2nd → FV   Clears data stored on TVM keys

–$1,000 → PV

4 → N   The order of entry
            does not matter.
10 → I/Y

CPT → FV   = $1,464.10

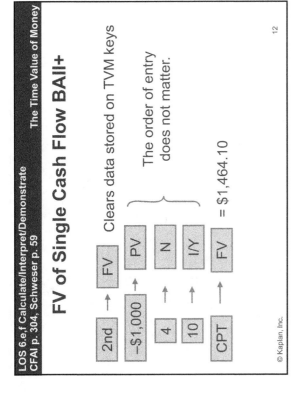

© Kaplan, Inc.

12

LOS 6.e,f Calculate/Interpret/Demonstrate The Time Value of Money
CFAI p. 304, Schweser p. 59

FV of Single Cash Flow BAII+

2nd → FV   Clears data stored on TVM keys

–$1,000 → PV

4 × 4 =16 → N   The order of entry
                    does not matter.
10 / 4 =2.5 → I/Y

CPT → FV   = $1,484.51

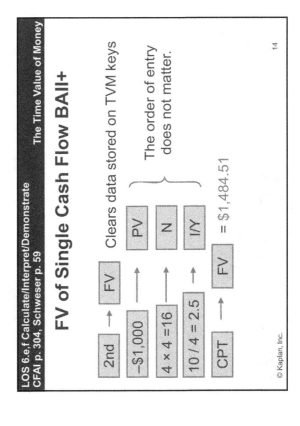

© Kaplan, Inc.

14

LOS 6.e,f Calculate/Interpret/Demonstrate
CFAI p. 304, Schweser p. 59
The Time Value of Money

Present Value of a Perpetuity

A preferred stock will pay $8 per year forever, and the rate of return is 10%. What is its present value?

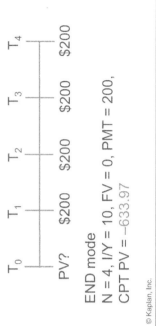

$i = 10\%$

PV?

$$PMT = \$8 = 10\% \times ?? \qquad PV = \frac{PMT}{r} = \frac{8}{0.1} = \$80$$

© Kaplan, Inc.

17 - 3

LOS 6.e,f Calculate/Interpret/Demonstrate
CFAI p. 304, Schweser p. 59
The Time Value of Money

Present Value of an Ordinary Annuity

What is the present value of $200 to be received at the end of each year for four years when the interest rate is 10%?

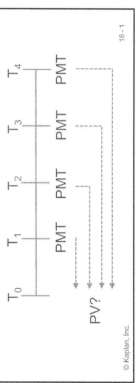

PV? $200 $200 $200 $200

END mode
N = 4, I/Y = 10, FV = 0, PMT = 200,
CPT PV = –633.97

© Kaplan, Inc.

19 - 1

LOS 6.e,f Calculate/Interpret/Demonstrate
The Time Value of Money
CFAI p. 304, Schweser p. 59

PV of a Single Sum BAII+

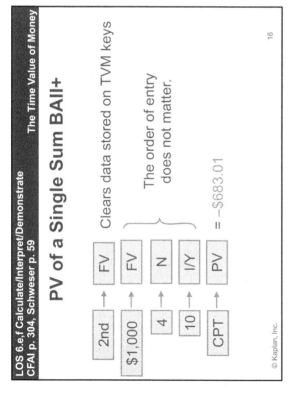

2nd → FV   Clears data stored on TVM keys

$1,000 → FV

4 → N   The order of entry
                does not matter.

10 → I/Y

CPT → PV   = –$683.01

© Kaplan, Inc.

16

LOS 6.e,f Calculate/Interpret/Demonstrate
CFAI p. 304, Schweser p. 59
The Time Value of Money

Present Value of an Ordinary Annuity

Ordinary annuity: A stream of equal CFs at equal intervals paid at end of each period

Set the calculator to END mode as cash flows are at the end of each period.

PV?   PMT   PMT   PMT   PMT

© Kaplan, Inc.

18 - 1

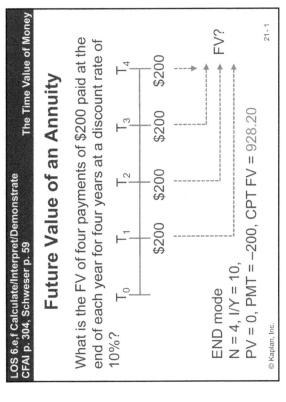

LOS 6.e,f Calculate/Interpret/Demonstrate
CFAI p. 304, Schweser p. 59

The Time Value of Money

PV of an Ordinary Annuity BAII+

Clears data stored on TVM keys

The order of entry does not matter.

2nd → FV
$200 → PMT
4 → N
10 → I/Y
CPT → PV

= –$633.97

© Kaplan, Inc.

20

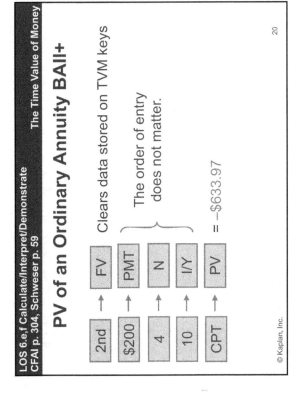

LOS 6.e,f Calculate/Interpret/Demonstrate
CFAI p. 304, Schweser p. 59

The Time Value of Money

Future Value of an Annuity

What is the FV of four payments of $200 paid at the end of each year for four years at a discount rate of 10%?

$$T_0 \quad T_1 \quad T_2 \quad T_3 \quad T_4$$

$200 $200 $200 $200

FV?

END mode
N = 4, I/Y = 10,
PV = 0, PMT = –200, CPT FV = 928.20

© Kaplan, Inc.

21-1

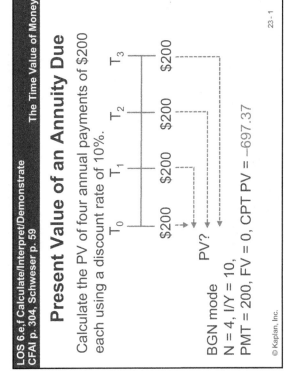

LOS 6.e,f Calculate/Interpret/Demonstrate
CFAI p. 304, Schweser p. 59

The Time Value of Money

Future Value of an Annuity BAII+

Clears data stored on TVM keys

The order of entry does not matter.

2nd → FV
–200 → PMT
4 → N
10 → I/Y
CPT → FV

= 928.20

© Kaplan, Inc.

22

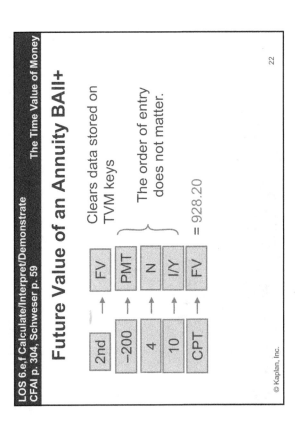

LOS 6.e,f Calculate/Interpret/Demonstrate
CFAI p. 304, Schweser p. 59

The Time Value of Money

Present Value of an Annuity Due

Calculate the PV of four annual payments of $200 each using a discount rate of 10%.

$$T_0 \quad T_1 \quad T_2 \quad T_3$$

$200 $200 $200 $200

PV?

BGN mode
N = 4, I/Y = 10,
PMT = 200, FV = 0, CPT PV = –697.37

© Kaplan, Inc.

23-1

Future Value of an Annuity Due

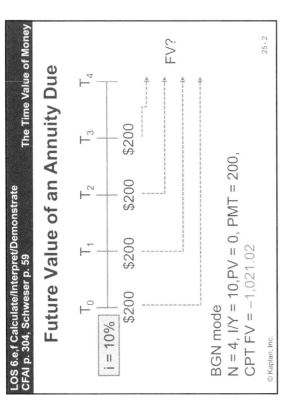

i = 10%

	T₀	T₁	T₂	T₃	T₄

$200 $200 $200 $200

FV?

BGN mode
N = 4, I/Y = 10, PV = 0, PMT = 200,
CPT FV = –1,021.02

© Kaplan, Inc.   25 - 2

END/BGN with Annuities

In **END** mode, the computed:

PV is for **one period before** the first payment

FV is **on the date of** the last payment

In **BGN** mode, the computed:

PV is **on the date of** the first payment

FV is for **one period after** the last payment

© Kaplan, Inc.   27

PV of an Annuity Due BAII+

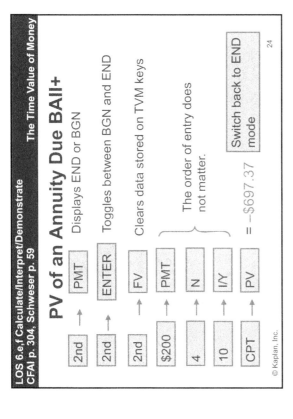

2nd	PMT	Displays END or BGN
2nd	ENTER	Toggles between BGN and END
2nd	FV	Clears data stored on TVM keys

$200 PMT
4   N
10   I/Y
CPT   PV

The order of entry does not matter.

= –$697.37

Switch back to END mode

© Kaplan, Inc.   24

FV of an Annuity Due BAII+

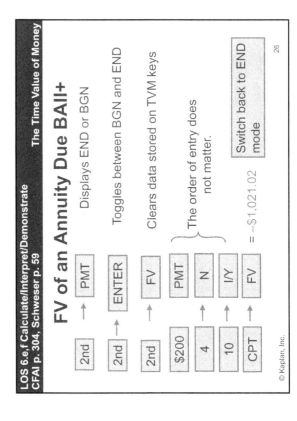

2nd	PMT	Displays END or BGN
2nd	ENTER	Toggles between BGN and END
2nd	FV	Clears data stored on TVM keys

$200 PMT
4   N
10   I/Y
CPT   FV

The order of entry does not matter.

= –$1,021.02

Switch back to END mode

© Kaplan, Inc.   26

Slide 28

Present Value of a Deferred Annuity

Compute the present value of an annuity of four annual $200 payments that begin five years from today, using a discount rate of 10%.

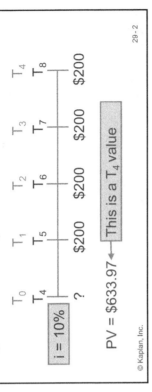

i = 10%

?

$200 $200 $200 $200

28

Slide 29-2

Present Value of a Deferred Annuity

2-step process:

1st Step: Calculate the present value in END mode to get the value at T_4

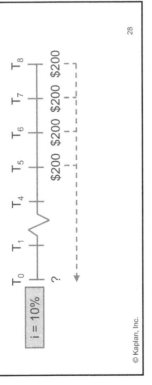

i = 10%

T_4
? $200 $200 $200 $200

PV = $633.97 ← This is a T_4 value

29 - 2

Slide 30-2

Present Value of a Deferred Annuity

2-step process:

2nd Step: Discount the T_4 value to a T_0 value

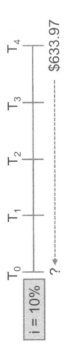

i = 10%

T_0 T_1 T_2 T_3 T_4
? $633.97

$$PV = \$433.01 = \frac{\$633.97}{\left(1 + 0.1\right)^4}$$

30 - 2

Slide 31

Calculating I/Y

Elmer has won his state lottery and has been offered 20 annual payments of $200,000 each beginning today or a single payment of $2,267,000.

What is the annual discount rate used to calculate the single-payment amount?

Note: Because the first payment is today, use BGN mode.

31

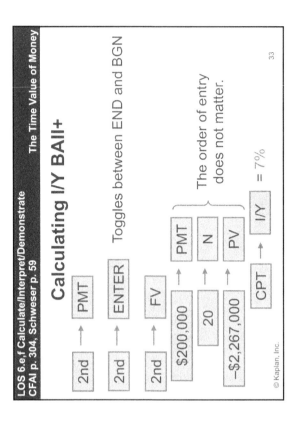

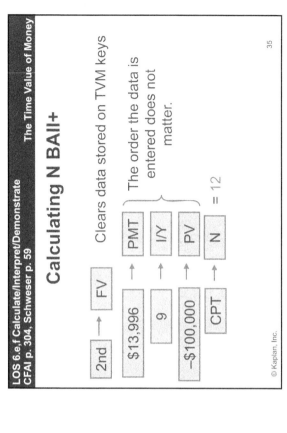

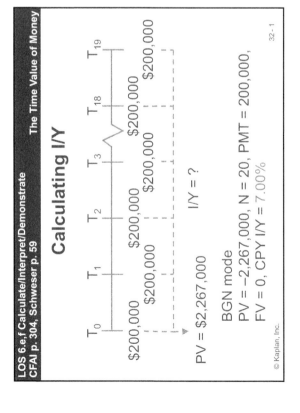

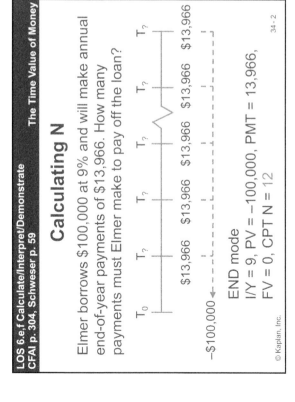

LOS 6.e,f Calculate/Interpret/Demonstrate
CFAI p. 304, Schweser p. 59   The Time Value of Money

Example: Retirement Savings

A client has $75,000 in savings now, will retire 20 years from today, and needs 25 payments of $62,000/year to begin then. Rate of return is 7%. What annual deposit must she make at the end of each year for 20 years to reach her goal?

© Kaplan, Inc.   36

LOS 6.e,f Calculate/Interpret/Demonstrate
CFAI p. 304, Schweser p. 59   The Time Value of Money

Example: Retirement Savings

Step 2: What annual deposit must she make at the end of each year?

T_0 T_1 T_2 T_3 T_{19} T_{20}

75,000   PMT   PMT   PMT   PMT   PMT   PMT

FV = −773,099

END mode
N = 20, I/Y = 7, PV = 75,000, FV = −773,099,
CPT PMT = 11,779

© Kaplan, Inc.   38 - 2

LOS 6.e,f Calculate/Interpret/Demonstrate
CFAI p. 304, Schweser p. 59   The Time Value of Money

Example: Retirement Savings

Step 1: How much is needed at T = 20 to fund retirement?

T_{20} T_{21} T_{22} T_{23} T_{43} T_{44}

$62,000 $62,000 $62,000 $62,000 $62,000 $62,000 $62,000

BGN mode
N = 25, I/Y = 7, FV = 0, PMT = 62,000,
CPT PV = −773,099

© Kaplan, Inc.   37 - 2

The Time Value of Money

Example: Retirement Savings

Over the last five years the EPS for Randall Corp. have been $4.00, $4.95, $5.15, $6.05, and $7.00. Calculate the compound annual rate of dividend growth over this period.

© Kaplan, Inc.   39 - 2

Slide 1

Quantitative Methods: Basic Concepts

7. Discounted Cash Flow Applications

KAPLAN UNIVERSITY | SCHOOL OF PROFESSIONAL AND CONTINUING EDUCATION | SCHWESER

Slide 2

Additional Learning Outcomes

LOS 6.a: interpreting interest rates

© Kaplan, Inc.

40

Slide 3

LOS 7.a Calculate/Interpret
CFAI p. 358, Schweser p. 96   Discounted Cash Flow Applications

Net Present Value (NPV)

The sum of the present values of a series of cash flows

$$NPV = CF_0 + \frac{CF_1}{(1+k)^1} + \frac{CF_2}{(1+k)^2} + \dots + \frac{CF_n}{(1+k)^n}$$

Discount rate = k

NPV ≥ 0 → accept project

NPV < 0 → reject project

© Kaplan, Inc.

42

Slide 4

LOS 7.a Calculate/Interpret
CFAI p. 358, Schweser p. 96   Discounted Cash Flow Applications

Net Present Value (NPV)

Example using a 9% discount rate

End of Year	Project X	Discounted Cash Flow
0	–$100	–$100.00
1	25	22.94
2	50	42.08
3	75	57.91
	NPV	$22.93

$$\frac{\$25}{(1.09)} = \$22.94$$

$$\frac{\$50}{(1.09)^2} = \$42.08$$

$$\frac{\$75}{(1.09)^3} = \$57.91$$

© Kaplan, Inc.

43 - 5

Net Present Value (NPV) BAII+

CF   Enters cash flow mode

2nd → CE/C   Clears data stored in memory

CF0= → −$100 → ENTER → ↓

C01= → $25 → ENTER → ↓

F01= → ↓

C02= → $50 → ENTER → ↓

© Kaplan, Inc.

44

Net Present Value (NPV) BAII+

F02= → ↑

C03= → $75 → ENTER → ↓

Enters Net Present Value mode

NPV

I= → 9 → ENTER → ↑

NPV= → CPT   = $22.93

© Kaplan, Inc.

45

Internal Rate of Return (IRR)

IRR is the discount rate that equates the PV of a series of cash flows to their cost

The IRR is the discount rate that makes the NPV = 0

$$NPV = 0 = CF_0 + \frac{CF_1}{(1+IRR)^1} + \frac{CF_2}{(1+IRR)^2} + \cdots + \frac{CF_n}{(1+IRR)^n}$$

© Kaplan, Inc.

46

Internal Rate of Return (IRR)

Example using a 19.4% discount rate

End of Year	Project X	Discounted Cash Flow
0	−$100	−$100.00
1	25	20.94
2	50	35.07
3	75	44.06
	NPV	$0*

$$\frac{\$25}{(1.194)} = \$20.94$$

$$\frac{\$50}{(1.194)^2} = \$35.07$$

$$\frac{\$75}{(1.194)^3} = \$44.06$$

© Kaplan, Inc.   *$0.07 due to rounding of discount factor

47 – 5

LOS 7.a Calculate/Interpret
CFAI p. 358, Schweser p. 96   Discounted Cash Flow Applications

Internal Rate of Return (IRR) BAII+

| CF | Enters cash flow mode |

| 2nd | → | CE/C | Clears data stored in memory |

CF0= → -$100 → ENTER → ↑ → →

C01= → $25 → ENTER → ↑ → →

F01= → → → ENTER → ↑

C02= → $50 → ENTER → ↑ → →

© Kaplan, Inc.

48

LOS 7.a Calculate/Interpret
CFAI p. 358, Schweser p. 96   Discounted Cash Flow Applications

Internal Rate of Return (IRR) BAII+

F02= → →

C03= → $75 → ENTER → →

IRR   Enters Internal Rate of Return mode

IRR= → CPT   = 19.438%

© Kaplan, Inc.

49

LOS 7.b Contrast
CFAI p. 362, Schweser p. 99   Discounted Cash Flow Applications

Possible Problems With IRR

1. When a series of cash flows has more than one change of sign, there can be more than one IRR

2. Comparing two projects, one can have higher NPV while the other has higher IRR

More on NPV and IRR in Corporate Finance

© Kaplan, Inc.

50

LOS 7.c Calculate/Interpret
CFAI p. 365, Schweser p. 101   Discounted Cash Flow Applications

Holding Period Return (HPR)

The percentage increase in wealth over a period

Price at end of period   Cash inflow

$$HPR = \frac{(P_1 - P_0) + CF_1}{P_0}$$

Price at start of period

$$HPR = \frac{Ending\ value}{Beginning\ value} - 1$$

© Kaplan, Inc.

51

LOS 7.c Calculate/Interpret
CFAI p. 365, Schweser p. 101   Discounted Cash Flow Applications

Holding Period Return (HPR)

1. An investment purchased nine months ago for $9 is now valued at $10.20. What is the holding period return?

9-month HPR:

$$HPR = \frac{\$10.20}{\$9} - 1 = 13.33\%$$

© Kaplan, Inc.   52 - 1

LOS 7.c Calculate/Interpret
CFAI p. 365, Schweser p. 101   Discounted Cash Flow Applications

Holding Period Return (HPR)

2. Stock purchased one year ago for $29 just paid a dividend of $1.30 and is valued at $30.50. What is the holding period (total) return?

12-month HPR:

$$HPR = \frac{(\$30.50 + \$1.30)}{\$29} - 1 = 9.66\%$$

© Kaplan, Inc.   53 - 1

LOS 7.c Calculate/Interpret
CFAI p. 365, Schweser p. 101   Discounted Cash Flow Applications

HPR and Effective Annual Yield (EAY)

An investor buys a stock for $20/sh. and sells it 9 months later for $22.50.

1. What is the (9-month) holding period yield?

$$HPR = \frac{(\$22.50 - \$20)}{\$20} = \frac{\$22.50}{\$20} - 1 = 12.5\%$$

2. What is the effective annual yield?

$$(1.125)^{12/9} - 1 \text{ or } \left(\frac{\$22.50}{\$20}\right)^{12/9} - 1 = 17\%$$

© Kaplan, Inc.   54 - 2

LOS 7.c Calculate/Interpret
CFAI p. 365, Schweser p. 101   Discounted Cash Flow Applications

HPR and Effective Annual Yield (EAY)

An investor buys a stock for $20/sh. and sells it 18 months later for $24 after collecting $1.10 in dividends.

1. What is the holding period return?

$$\frac{(\$24.00 + 1.10)}{\$20} - 1 = 25.5\%$$

2. What is the effective annual return?

$$(1.255)^{12/18} - 1 \text{ or } \left(\frac{\$25.10}{\$20}\right)^{12/18} - 1 = 16.3\%$$

© Kaplan, Inc.   55 - 2

LOS 7.d Calculate/Compare/Evaluate
CFAI p. 366, Schweser p. 101   Discounted Cash Flow Applications

Money-Weighted Returns

Money-weighted returns are like an IRR measure

$$CF_0 + \frac{CF_1}{1+MWR} + \cdots + \frac{CF_N}{(1+MWR)^N} = 0$$

Periods must be equal length, use <u>shortest period</u> with no significant cash flows

© Kaplan, Inc.

57

LOS 7.d Calculate/Compare/Evaluate
CFAI p. 366, Schweser p. 101   Discounted Cash Flow Applications

Time-Weighted Return Example

Step 2: Compute effective annual compound return

$$TWR = \left[(1.2444)(1.1355) \right]^{1/2} - 1 = 18.87\%$$

Note: We have two years of returns, so we take the square root to get annual compound rate.

© Kaplan, Inc.

59 - 1

LOS 7.d Calculate/Compare/Evaluate
CFAI p. 366, Schweser p. 101   Discounted Cash Flow Applications

Time-Weighted Returns

Annual time-weighted returns are effective annual compound returns.

$$TWR = \left[\left(\frac{End\ Value_1}{Begin\ Value_1} \right) \left(\frac{End\ Value_2}{Begin\ Value_2} \right) \cdots \left(\frac{End\ Value_N}{Begin\ Value_N} \right) \right]^{\frac{1}{\#YEARS}} - 1$$

Number of years not necessarily number of holding periods

Holding periods can be any length

Calculate HPRs for periods between significant cash flows

© Kaplan, Inc.

56

LOS 7.d Calculate/Compare/Evaluate
CFAI p. 366, Schweser p. 101   Discounted Cash Flow Applications

Time-Weighted Return Example

Jan.1, 20X1: buys 200 shares XYZ for $135 per share.

Jan.1, 20X2: receives dividend of $13 per share, sells 100 shares for $155 per share, does not reinvest dividends.

Jan.1, 20X3: receives dividend of $14 per share and share price is $162.

What is the investor's <u>annual</u> time-weighted return?

Step 1: Compute HPRs

$$\frac{(\$155 + \$13)}{\$135} - 1 = 24.44\% \qquad \frac{(\$162 + \$14)}{\$155} - 1 = 13.55\%$$

© Kaplan, Inc.

58 - 2

Reference Level I CFA Curriculum,
Reading 7, Problem 9   Discounted Cash Flow Applications

MWR Practice Problem

An investor buys a share for $1,000 at t=0 (in years)

t=1: receives a dividend of $25 and purchases three more shares at $1,055 each

t=2: receives dividends totalling $100 and sells all shares for $1,100 each

What is the investor's annual money-weighted return?

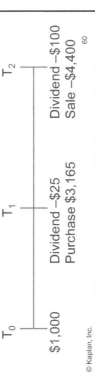

T_0 T_1 T_2

$1,000   Dividend –$25   Dividend –$100
            Purchase $3,165   Sale –$4,400

© Kaplan, Inc.   60

Reference Level I CFA Curriculum,
Reading 7, Problem 9   Discounted Cash Flow Applications

MWR Practice Problem

CF   Enters cash flow mode

2nd → CE/C   Clears data stored in memory

CF0= → 1,000 → ENTER → ↓

C01= → 3,140 → ENTER → ↓

F01= → ↓ → ENTER → ↓

C02= → –4,400 → ENTER → ↓

© Kaplan, Inc.   61

Reference Level I CFA Curriculum,
Reading 7, Problem 9   Discounted Cash Flow Applications

MWR Practice Problem

IRR   Enters Internal Rate of Return mode

IRR= → CPT   = 6.91%

We used annual cash flows, so our IRR is the annual compound rate of return.

Had we used quarterly cash flows to get a quarterly IRR, we would need to convert to an annual rate.

© Kaplan, Inc.   62

LOS 7.e Calculate/Interpret
CFAI p. 372, Schweser p. 105   Discounted Cash Flow Applications

BDY, HPY, EAY, MMY

Bank discount yield $= \dfrac{\text{Discount}}{\text{Face}} \times \dfrac{360}{\text{days to maturity}}$

Holding period yield $= \dfrac{\text{Ending value}}{\text{Beginning value}} - 1$

Effective annual yield $= (1+\text{HPY})^{\frac{365}{\text{days}}} - 1$

Money market yield $= \text{HPY} \times \dfrac{360}{\text{days to maturity}}$

© Kaplan, Inc.   63

Slide 1

LOS 7.e Calculate/Interpret
CFAI p. 372, Schweser p. 105   Discounted Cash Flow Applications

Money Market Yields

A 90-day T-bill is purchased for $997.40. What are the discount yield, holding period yield, money market yield, and the effective yield?

Discount yield: $\dfrac{\$2.60}{\$1,000} \times \dfrac{360}{90} = 1.04\%$

90-day HPY: $\dfrac{\$1,000}{\$997.40} - 1 = 0.2607\%$

Money market yield: $0.2607 \times \dfrac{360}{90} = 1.0428\%$

Effective annual yield: $(1.002607)^{\frac{365}{90}} - 1 = 1.0615\%$

© Kaplan, Inc.

65 - 4

Slide 2

Quantitative Methods

Quantitative Methods: Basic Concepts

8. Statistical Concepts and Market Returns

KAPLAN UNIVERSITY SCHOOL OF PROFESSIONAL AND CONTINUING EDUCATION | SCHWESER

Slide 3

LOS 7.e Calculate/Interpret
CFAI p. 372, Schweser p. 105   Discounted Cash Flow Applications

Yields for 90-day T-bill Priced at $980

$BDY = \dfrac{20}{1,000} \times \dfrac{360}{90} = 8\%$ [Simple annualized discount]

$HPY = \dfrac{1,000}{980} - 1 = 2.04\%$ [90-day HPY]

$EAY = (1.0204)^{\frac{365}{90}} - 1 = 8.53\%$ [Effective rate]

$MMY = 0.0204 \times \dfrac{360}{90} = 8.16\%$ [Simple annualized]

© Kaplan, Inc.

64

Slide 4

LOS 7.f Convert
CFAI p. 372, Schweser p. 108   Discounted Cash Flow Applications

Converting Between Yield Measures

A money market security with 173 days to maturity has a money market yield of 4.53%. What is its EAY?

$MMY = HPY \times \dfrac{360}{\text{days to maturity}}$

$HPY = 4.53\% \times \dfrac{173}{360}$

$= 2.177\%$

$\therefore HPY = MMY \times \dfrac{\text{days to maturity}}{360}$

$EAY = (1 + HPY)^{\frac{365}{\text{days}}} - 1$

$EAY = (1 + 0.02177)^{\frac{365}{173}} - 1 = 4.649\%$

© Kaplan, Inc.

66 - 3

LOS 8.a Distinguish
CFAI p. 388, Schweser p. 121

Measurement Scales (NOIR)

- Nominal – only names make sense
    (e.g., robin, parrot, seagull)

- Ordinal – order makes sense
    (e.g., large-cap, mid-cap, small-cap)

- Interval – intervals make sense
    (e.g., 40°F is 10° greater than 30°F)

- Ratio – ratios make sense (absolute zero)
    (e.g., $200 is twice as much as $100)

© Kaplan, Inc.

68

LOS 8.c Calculate/Interpret
CFAI p. 392, Schweser p. 123

Describing Data or Distribution

Measures of central tendency
- Mean (arithmetic, geometric, harmonic)
- Median, ½ higher and ½ lower
- Mode, most frequent outcome

Measures of dispersion
- Standard deviation, variance
- Range, highest to lowest
- MAD, mean absolute deviation

© Kaplan, Inc.

69

LOS 8.c Calculate/Interpret
CFAI p. 392, Schweser p. 123

Describing a Statistical Distribution

A relative frequency distribution shows the percentage of a distribution's outcomes in each interval

A cumulative frequency distribution shows the percentage of observations less than the upper bound of each interval

© Kaplan, Inc.

70

LOS 8.d Describe
CFAI p. 397, Schweser p. 126

Histogram

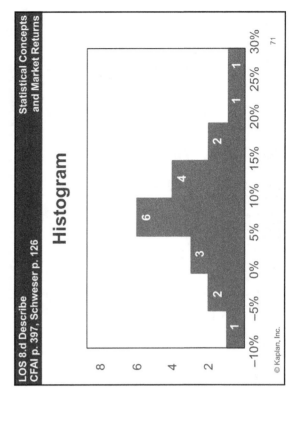

© Kaplan, Inc.

71

LOS 8.d Describe
CFAI p. 397, Schweser p. 126

Statistical Concepts
and Market Returns

Relative Frequency

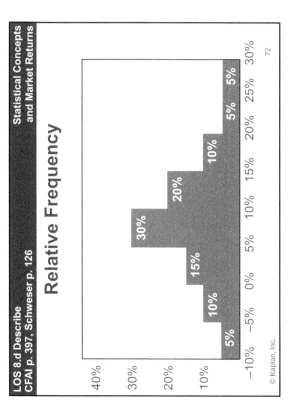

© Kaplan, Inc.

72

LOS 8.d Describe
CFAI p. 397, Schweser p. 126

Statistical Concepts
and Market Returns

Cumulative Relative Frequency

© Kaplan, Inc.

73

LOS 8.e Calculate/Interpret
CFAI p. 402, Schweser p. 127

Statistical Concepts
and Market Returns

Arithmetic and Geometric Means

A mutual fund had the following returns over 5 years:
6%, 11%, −3%, 8%, 15%.

1. What is the average annual return?

$$\text{Arithmetic mean} = \frac{6\% + 11\% + 3\% + 8\% + 5\%}{5} = 7.4\%$$

2. What is the equivalent compound annual rate of return?

$$\text{Geometric mean} = \left[(1.06)(1.11)(0.97)(1.08)(1.15)\right]^{\frac{1}{5}} - 1 = 7.23\%$$

© Kaplan, Inc.

74 - 2

LOS 8.e Calculate/Interpret
CFAI p. 402, Schweser p. 127

Statistical Concepts
and Market Returns

Weighted Mean

Asset allocation in an investment account: Cash 10%, Stock 35%, Bonds 55%

Annual returns: Cash = 2%, Stock = 16%, Bonds 8%

What is the account return for the year?

Asset	Weight	Return	Weighted Return
Cash	10%	2%	0.2%
Stock	35%	16%	5.6%
Bonds	55%	8%	4.4%
	100%		10.2%

© Kaplan, Inc.

75 - 4

Harmonic Mean

Investor buys $3,000 of a stock at the end of Month 1 at $20 a share, and $3,000 at the end of Month 2 at $25 per share.

What is the average cost per share of stock?

$$\frac{N}{\sum\limits_{i=1}^{N}\dfrac{1}{X_i}} = \overline{X}_{Harmonic}$$

$$= \frac{2(3,000)}{\dfrac{3,000}{20} + \dfrac{3,000}{25}}$$

$$= \frac{2}{\dfrac{1}{20} + \dfrac{1}{25}} = \$22.22\,\text{per share}$$

© Kaplan, Inc.

76 - 3

Comparing Means

Calculate the arithmetic, geometric, and harmonic means of 2, 3, and 4.

Arithmetic: $\dfrac{2+3+4}{3} = 3$

Largest

Geometric: $\sqrt[3]{2 \times 3 \times 4} = 2.88$

Harmonic: $\dfrac{3}{\dfrac{1}{2} + \dfrac{1}{3} + \dfrac{1}{4}} = 2.77$

Smallest

© Kaplan, Inc.

77 - 4

Median

Midpoint of a data set, **half above and half below**

- With an <u>odd number</u> of observations
  - 2, 5, 7, 11, 14   Median = 7
- With an <u>even number</u> of observations, median is the average of the two middle observations
  - 3, 9, 10, 20 ⟶ Median = (9 + 10) / 2 = 9.5

Less affected by extreme values than the mean

© Kaplan, Inc.

78

Mode

Value occurring most frequently in a data set

2, 4, 5, 5, 7, *8*, *8*, *8*, 10, 12   Mode = 8

Data sets can have more than one mode (bimodal, trimodal, etc.)

© Kaplan, Inc.

79

Quantiles

75% of the data points are less than the 3rd quartile

60% of the data points are less than the 60th percentile (6th decile)

$$\text{Percentile position}_y = (n+1)\frac{y}{100}$$

–3   0   5   5   7   11   17   18   20   23   29

With 11 observations, the 70th **percentile** position is **(11 + 1) × 0.70 = 8.4**; 18 + 0.4(20 – 18) = 18.8

© Kaplan, Inc.

80

Range and Mean Absolute Deviation

Given annual returns data: 15%, –5%, 12%, 22%

1. What is the data's range?

Range = 22% – (–5%) = 27%

2. What is the data's mean absolute deviation?

$$\text{Mean} = \frac{(15 - 5 + 12 + 22)}{4} = 11\%$$

$$\text{MAD} = \frac{\left(|15 - 11| + |-5 - 11| + |12 - 11| + |22 - 11|\right)}{4} = 8\%$$

© Kaplan, Inc.

81-2

Population Variance and Standard Deviation

Variance is the average of the squared deviations from the mean

Standard deviation is the square root of variance

$$\sigma^2 = \frac{\sum_{i=1}^{N}(X_i - \mu)^2}{N} \qquad \sigma = \sqrt{\sigma^2}$$

© Kaplan, Inc.

82

Sample Variance (s²) and Sample Standard Deviation (s)

$$s^2 = \frac{\sum_{i=1}^{n}(X_i - \overline{X})^2}{n-1} \qquad s = \sqrt{\frac{\sum_{i=1}^{n}(X_i - \overline{X})^2}{n-1}}$$

Note that for sample variance, the sum of the squared deviations is **divided by n – 1 instead of *n***

© Kaplan, Inc.

83

Slide (top left):

LOS 8.g Calculate/Interpret
CFAI p. 426, Schweser p. 133

Statistical Concepts
and Market Returns

Variance and Std Dev BAII+

2nd → 7 — Enters data entry mode

2nd → CE/C — Clears data stored in memory

X01 = → 0.15 → ENTER → ↓

Y01 = → ↓ — This is used for entering the probability of the X variable occurring; as we are using historic data, this can be left blank.

X02 = → -0.05 → ENTER → ↓

Y02 = → ↓

© Kaplan, Inc.

85

Slide (bottom left):

LOS 8.g Calculate/Interpret
CFAI p. 426, Schweser p. 133

Statistical Concepts
and Market Returns

Calculating Variance (σ^2)

Returns for a stock over four years are 15%, –5%, 12%, and 22%. Estimate the annual standard deviation of returns.

Sample Mean $\bar{X} = \dfrac{15 - 5 + 12 + 22}{4} = 11\%$

$S_x^2 = \dfrac{(15-11)^2 + (-5-11)^2 + (12-11)^2 + (22-11)^2}{4-1} = 131.3$

$S_x = \sqrt{131.3} = 11.46\%$

© Kaplan, Inc.

84 - 3

Slide (top right):

LOS 8.h Calculate/Interpret
CFAI p. 437, Schweser p. 137

Statistical Concepts
and Market Returns

Chebyshev's Inequality

Specifies the **minimum percentage** of observations that lie **within** k standard deviations of the mean; applies to any distribution with $k > 1$

Min.% is $1 - \dfrac{1}{k^2}$

Min. % for 2 std. dev = $1 - \dfrac{1}{2^2} = 1 - \dfrac{1}{4} = 75\%$

© Kaplan, Inc.

87 - 1

Slide (bottom right):

LOS 8.g Calculate/Interpret
CFAI p. 426, Schweser p. 133

Statistical Concepts
and Market Returns

Variance and Std Dev BAII+

X03 = → 0.12 → ENTER → ↓

Y03 = → ↓

X04 = → 0.22 → ENTER → ↓

2nd → 8

2nd → ENTER — Enters statistics mode

↓ — Keep pressing until **1-V** appears

1-V = 1 Variable

Pressing the down arrow repeatedly now allows you to review the statistic for the data you entered.

© Kaplan, Inc.

86

LOS 8.i Calculate/Interpret
CFAI p. 439, Schweser p. 138

Coefficient of Variation (CV)

A measure of risk per unit of return

Example:	Mean	σ
Asset A	5%	10%
Asset B	8%	12%

Asset B has higher std. dev. and higher return
Lower CV is better, less risk per unit of return

$$CV = \frac{s}{\overline{X}} \qquad CV_A = \frac{10}{5} = 2.0 \qquad CV_B = \frac{12}{8} = 1.5$$

© Kaplan, Inc.

88 - 1

LOS 8.i Calculate/Interpret
CFAI p. 439, Schweser p. 138

Sharpe Ratio

Excess return per unit of risk (CV measures risk per unit of return); **higher is better**

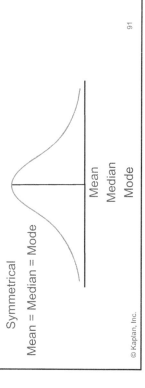

$$Sharpe\ ratio = \frac{\overline{R}_P - \overline{R}_F}{\sigma_P}$$

Mean portfolio return = 17%, standard deviation = 9%, average risk-free rate = 5%.
What is the Sharpe ratio for the portfolio?

$$Sharpe\ ratio = \frac{17 - 5}{9} = 1.33$$

89 - 1

LOS 8.i Calculate/Interpret
CFAI p. 439, Schweser p. 138

CV and Sharpe Ratio

Rf = 4%	Port A	Port B	Port C
Return	8%	13%	17%
σ	5%	9%	11%

1. Which portfolio is preferred based on their CV?

$$CV_A = \frac{5\%}{8\%} = 0.625 \quad CV_B = \frac{9\%}{13\%} = 0.692 \quad CV_c = \frac{11\%}{17\%} = 0.647$$

2. Which portfolio is preferred based on their Sharpe ratios?

$$SR_A = \frac{(8-4)}{5} = 0.8 \quad SR_B = \frac{(13-4)}{9} = 1.0 \quad SR_B = \frac{(17-4)}{11} = 1.2$$

© Kaplan, Inc.

90 - 2

LOS 8.j,k Explain/Describe
CFAI p. 444, Schweser p. 140

Skewness

- Skew measures the degree to which a distribution lacks symmetry
  - A symmetrical distribution has skew = 0

Symmetrical

Mean = Median = Mode

Mean
Median
Mode

© Kaplan, Inc.

91

LOS 8.j,k Explain/Describe
CFAI p. 444, Schweser p. 140

Statistical Concepts and Market Returns

Positive Skew = Right Skew

- Positive skew has outliers in the right tail
- Skew absolute values > 0.5 are significant
- Mean is most affected by outliers

"Pull" on right tail to get positive/right skew

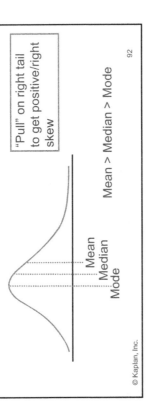

Mean > Median > Mode

Mean
Median
Mode

© Kaplan, Inc.

92

LOS 8.j,k Explain/Describe
CFAI p. 444, Schweser p. 140

Statistical Concepts and Market Returns

Negative Skew = Left Skew

- Negative skew has outliers in the left tail
- Mean is most affected by outliers

"Median is in the middle"

Mean
Median
Mode

Mean < Median < Mode

© Kaplan, Inc.

93

LOS 8.l Explain
CFAI p. 447, Schweser p. 141

Statistical Concepts and Market Returns

Kurtosis

- Measures the degree to which a distribution is more or less peaked than a normal distribution
- *Leptokurtic* (kurtosis > 3) is **more peaked** with **fatter tails** (more extreme outliers)

Leptokurtic

Higher kurtosis = Higher probability in tails

Normal Distribution

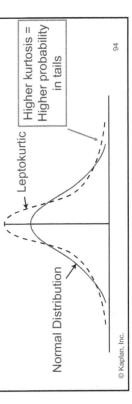

© Kaplan, Inc.

94

LOS 8.l Explain
CFAI p. 447, Schweser p. 141

Statistical Concepts and Market Returns

Kurtosis

- **Kurtosis for a normal distribution is 3.0**
- **Excess** kurtosis is kurtosis minus 3
- **Excess** kurtosis is *0 for a normal distribution*
- **Excess** kurtosis greater than 1.0 in absolute value is considered significant

© Kaplan, Inc.

95

LOS 8.m Compare
CFAI p. 454, Schweser p. 143

**Statistical Concepts
and Market Returns**

Arithmetic vs. Geometric Mean

Arithmetic mean annual return is expectation (best guess) of returns for any single year.

Geometric mean is estimate of average annual compound returns over multiple periods.

96

CFA Curriculum Vol. 1,
R.8, Q.22, p. 465

Two portfolios have unimodal return distributions. Portfolio 1 has a skewness of 0.77, and Portfolio 2 has a skewness of –1.11.

Which of the following is correct?

A. For Portfolio 1, the median is less than the mean.

B. For Portfolio 1, the mode is greater than the mean.

C. For Portfolio 2, the mean is greater than the median.

97 - 2

**Statistical Concepts
and Market Returns**

Additional Learning Outcomes

LOS 8.a: descriptive and inferential statistics, population vs. sample

LOS 8.b: parameters, sample statistics, and frequency distributions

98

Quantitative Methods

Quantitative Methods: Basic Concepts

9. Probability Concepts

KAPLAN UNIVERSITY   SCHOOL OF PROFESSIONAL AND CONTINUING EDUCATION | SCHWESER

Types of Probability

Empirical: Based on analysis of data

Subjective: Based on personal perception

A priori: Based on reasoning, not experience

© Kaplan, Inc.

101

Joint Probability

The probability that **both** of two events will occur is their joint probability

Example using conditional probability:

P (interest rates will increase) = P(I) = 40%

P (recession *given* a rate increase) = P(R|I) = 70%

Probability of a recession **and** an increase in rates,
P(RI) = P(R|I) × P(I) = 0.7 × 0.4 = 28%

© Kaplan, Inc.

103

Two Properties of Probability

Probability of an event, $P(E_i)$, is between 0 and 1

$$0 \leq P(E_i) \leq 1$$

For a set of events that are mutually exclusive and exhaustive, the **sum of probabilities is 1**

$$\Sigma P(E_i) = 1$$

© Kaplan, Inc.

100

Conditional vs. Unconditional

Two types of probability:

Unconditional: P(A), the probability of an event regardless of the outcomes of other events (e.g., probability market will be up for the day)

Conditional: P(A|B), the probability of A given that B has occurred (e.g., probability that the market will be up for the day, given that the Fed raises interest rates)

© Kaplan, Inc.

102

Joint Probability of Any Number of Independent Events

Dependent events: Knowing the outcome of one tells you something about the probability of the other

Independent events: Occurrence of one event does not influence the occurrence of the other.

For the joint probability of independent events, just multiply

Example: Flipping a fair coin, P (heads) = 50%
The probability of 3 heads in succession is simply:
$0.5 \times 0.5 \times 0.5 = 0.5^3 = 0.125$, or 12.5%

© Kaplan, Inc.   105

Conditional and Unconditional Probabilities

Joint probabilities

© Kaplan, Inc.   107 - 4

Probability That at Least One of Two Events Will Occur

P(A or B) = P(A) + P(B) − P(AB)
We must subtract the joint probability P(AB)

Don't double count P(AB)

P(A)

P(B)

P(AB)

© Kaplan, Inc.   104

Conditional and Unconditional Probabilities

P (Interest rate increase) = P(I) = 40%

P (Recession | Increase) = P(R|I) = 0.70

P (Recession | No Increase) = P(R|I^C) = 0.10

What is the (unconditional) probability of recession?

P(R) = P(R|I) × P(I) + P(R|I^C) × P(I^C)

= $0.70 \times 0.40 + 0.10 \times 0.60 = 0.34$

© Kaplan, Inc.   106 - 1

Conditional Probability Example

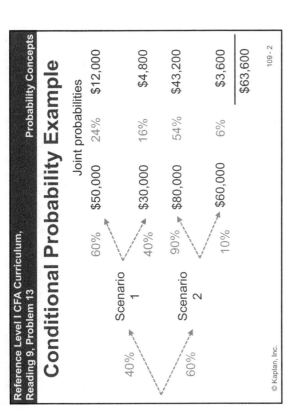

Joint probabilities

	$50,000	24%	$12,000
Scenario 1			
	$30,000	16%	$4,800
	$80,000	54%	$43,200
Scenario 2			
	$60,000	6%	$3,600
			$63,600

© Kaplan, Inc.   109 - 2

Conditional Probability Example

Recovery of $100,000 defaulted loan

Scenario	Prob.	$Recovered	Prob.
#1	40%	50,000	60%
		30,000	40%
#2	60%	80,000	90%
		60,000	10%

Calculate the expected recovery amount.

$0.4(0.6 \times 50 + 0.4 \times 30) + 0.6(0.9 \times 80 + 0.1 \times 60) =$
$0.4(30 + 12) + 0.6(72 + 6) = \$63,600$

© Kaplan, Inc.   108 - 1

Expected Value, Conditional Expectations

Using the probabilities from the tree:

Expected(EPS) = $1.51
$= 0.18(1.80) + 0.42(1.70) + 0.24(1.30) + 0.16(1.00)$

Conditional expectations of EPS:

E(EPS)|GDP growth > 3% =
$0.30(1.80) + 0.70(1.70) = \$1.73$

E(EPS)| GDP growth ≤ 3% =
$0.60(1.30) + 0.40(1.00) = \$1.18$

© Kaplan, Inc.   111 - 2

An Investment Tree

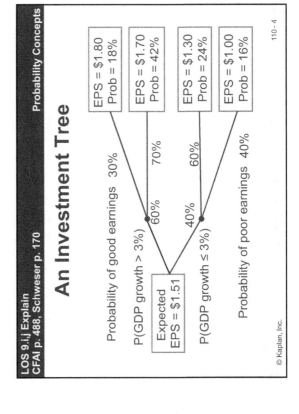

Probability of good earnings   30%

P(GDP growth > 3%)

Expected
EPS = $1.51

P(GDP growth ≤ 3%)

Probability of poor earnings   40%

| EPS = $1.80 |
| Prob = 18% |

| EPS = $1.70 |
| Prob = 42% |

| EPS = $1.30 |
| Prob = 24% |

| EPS = $1.00 |
| Prob = 16% |

© Kaplan, Inc.   110 - 4

Covariance

LOS 9.k Calculate/Interpret
CFAI p. 495, Schweser p. 171 — Probability Concepts

Covariance: A measure of how two variables move together

- Values range from minus infinity to plus infinity
- Units of covariance are difficult to interpret
- Covariance is positive when the two variables tend to be above (below) their expected values at the same time

For each observation, multiply each probability by the product of the two random variables' deviations from their means, and sum them

© Kaplan, Inc.

112

Correlation

LOS 9.k Calculate/Interpret
CFAI p. 495, Schweser p. 171 — Probability Concepts

$Cov_{AB} = 0.0046$, $\sigma_A = 0.0623$, $\sigma_B = 0.0991$

What is the correlation between the two assets?

$$\rho_{AB} = \frac{Cov_{AB}}{\sigma_A \sigma_B} = \frac{0.0046}{0.0623 \times 0.0991} = 0.745$$

© Kaplan, Inc.

113 - 1

Expected Return, Variance, and Standard Deviation (Probability Model)

LOS 9.l Calculate/Interpret
CFAI p. 495, Schweser p. 174 — Probability Concepts

Expected Value: $E(X) = \Sigma P(x_i)x_i$

Economy	$P(x_i)$	Return (x_i)	$P(x_i)x_i$
Recession	0.25	−0.10	−0.025
Normal	0.50	0.08	0.040
Boom	0.25	0.22	0.055
			$E(X) = 0.070$

© Kaplan, Inc.

114 - 4

Expected Return, Variance, and Standard Deviation (Probability Model)

LOS 9.l Calculate/Interpret
CFAI p. 495, Schweser p. 174 — Probability Concepts

Variance: $\sigma^2_X = \Sigma P(x_i)[x_i - E(X)]^2$

Economy	$P(x_i)$	Return(x_i)	$P(x_i)x_i$	$P(x_i)[x_i - E(X)]^2$
Recession	0.25	−0.10	−0.025	0.00723
Normal	0.50	0.08	0.040	0.00005
Boom	0.25	0.22	0.055	0.00563
			$E(X) = 0.070$	$0.01290 = \sigma^2$

Standard deviation: Square root of $\sigma^2 = 0.1136$

© Kaplan, Inc.

115 - 6

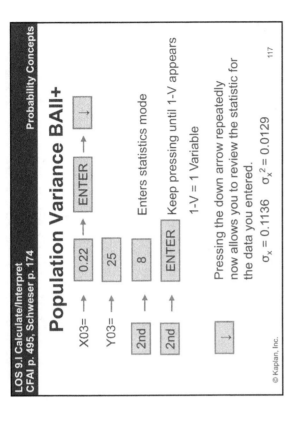

LOS 9.l Calculate/Interpret
CFAI p. 495, Schweser p. 174

Population Variance BAII+

2nd → 7 → Enters data entry mode

2nd → CE/C → Clears data stored in memory

X01= → -0.1 → ENTER → →

Y01= → 25 → ENTER → →

The calculator requires the probability to be entered as a whole number, not as a decimal.

X02= → 0.08 → ENTER → →

Y02= → 50 → ENTER → →

© Kaplan, Inc.

116

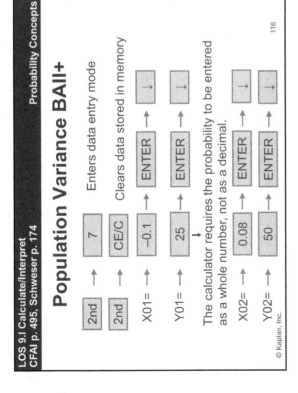

LOS 9.l Calculate/Interpret
CFAI p. 495, Schweser p. 174

Portfolio Variance and Standard Deviation

Portfolio variance also uses the weights of the assets in the portfolio, use either formula

$$Var(R_p) = \sigma_A^2 w_A^2 + \sigma_B^2 w_B^2 + 2w_A w_B Cov_{AB}$$

$$Note: Cov_{AB} = \rho_{AB}\sigma_A\sigma_B$$

$$Var(R_p) = \sigma_A^2 w_A^2 + \sigma_B^2 w_B^2 + 2w_A w_B \rho_{AB}\sigma_A\sigma_B$$

Also covered in Portfolio Management

© Kaplan, Inc.

118

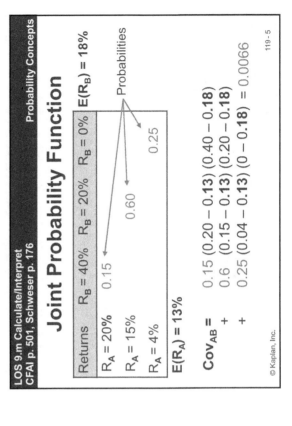

LOS 9.l Calculate/Interpret
CFAI p. 495, Schweser p. 174

Population Variance BAII+

X03= → 0.22 → ENTER → →

Y03= → 25 → →

2nd → 8 → Enters statistics mode

2nd → ENTER → Keep pressing until 1-V appears

1-V = 1 Variable

→ Pressing the down arrow repeatedly now allows you to review the statistic for the data you entered.

$$\sigma_x = 0.1136 \qquad \sigma_x^2 = 0.0129$$

© Kaplan, Inc.

117

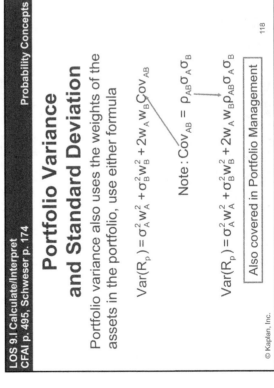

LOS 9.m Calculate/Interpret
CFAI p. 501, Schweser p. 176

Joint Probability Function

$$E(R_B) = 18\%$$

Returns	$R_B = 40\%$	$R_B = 20\%$	$R_B = 0\%$
$R_A = 20\%$	0.15		
$R_A = 15\%$		0.60	
$R_A = 4\%$			0.25

Probabilities

$$E(R_A) = 13\%$$

$$Cov_{AB} = \quad 0.15\,(0.20 - 0.13)\,(0.40 - 0.18)$$
$$+ \quad 0.6\;\;(0.15 - 0.13)\,(0.20 - 0.18)$$
$$+ \quad 0.25\,(0.04 - 0.13)\,(0 - 0.18) = 0.0066$$

© Kaplan, Inc.

119-5

Bayes' Formula

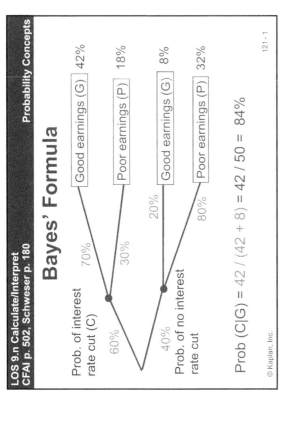

Prob. of interest rate cut (C)

Good earnings (G) 42%

Poor earnings (P) 18%

Good earnings (G) 8%

Poor earnings (P) 32%

70%

30%

20%

80%

60%

40%

Prob. of no interest rate cut

Prob (C|G) = 42 / (42 + 8) = 42 / 50 = 84%

© Kaplan, Inc.

121 - 1

Combination Formula

You have been asked to select 4 of 10 energy stocks in a portfolio to be sold to reduce exposure to that industry. How many different groups of four could you select?

$$_nC_r = \frac{n!}{(n-r)!r!} = \frac{10!}{(10-4)!\times 4!} = 210$$

BAII+: $10 \rightarrow 2^{nd} \rightarrow nCr \rightarrow 4 \rightarrow = 210$

+ button

© Kaplan, Inc.

123 - 2

Bayes' Formula

Given the following probability tree, what is the probability that a firm with good earnings, picked at random, would also have experienced an interest-rate cut?

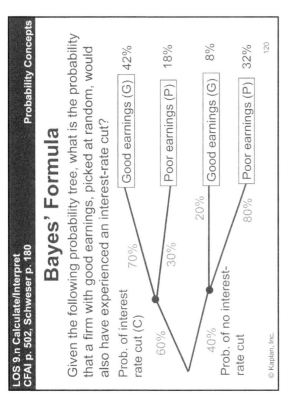

Prob. of interest rate cut (C)

Good earnings (G) 42%

Poor earnings (P) 18%

Good earnings (G) 8%

Poor earnings (P) 32%

70%

30%

20%

80%

60%

40%

Prob. of no interest-rate cut

© Kaplan, Inc.

120

Labeling

Out of 10 stocks, 5 will be rated buy, 3 will be rated hold, and 2 will be rated sell. How many ways are there to do this?

$$\frac{10!}{5!\times 3!\times 2!} = 2,520$$

© Kaplan, Inc.

122 - 1

Permutation Formula

You have 5 stocks and want to sell 3, one at a time.
How many ways are there to choose the 3 stocks to
sell in order?

$$\frac{5!}{(5-3)!} = 60$$

BAII+: $5 \rightarrow 2^{nd} \rightarrow nPr \rightarrow 3 \rightarrow = 60$

← button

© Kaplan, Inc.   124 - 2

Additional Learning Outcomes

LOS 9.a: defining probability terms

LOS 9.c: odds for and against

LOS 9.e multiplication, addition, and
            total probability rules

© Kaplan, Inc.   125

Additional Problems

KAPLAN UNIVERSITY SCHOOL OF PROFESSIONAL AND CONTINUING EDUCATION | **SCHWESER**

---

1) Key information about a two-asset portfolio is
   presented below:

Asset	Weight	Expected Return	Variance
J	0.60	15%	49
K	0.40	5%	36

Assets J and K have a correlation of 0.5714. What is
this portfolio's variance?

A. 11.52.
B. 34.92.
C. 43.80.

© Kaplan, Inc.   - 2

Additional Problems

2) Consider the following probability distribution for a company's profit margin for next year:

| Possible profit margin | Probability of profit margin |
X	P(X)
−7%	0.10
−3%	0.50
4%	0.40

What is the variance of this probability distribution?

A. 3.93.

B. 15.44.

C. 41.49.

- 5

Additional Problems

3) A 120-day Treasury bill has a money market yield of 3.25%. Its effective annual yield is *closest* to:

A. 3.28%.

B. 3.30%.

C. 3.33%.

- 3

Additional Problems

4) Cliff Corporation's dividends the past six years were $0.31, $0.12, $0.40, $0.50, $0.60, and $0.70. The compound annual rate of dividend growth over this period is *closest* to:

A. 14.5%.

B. 17.7%.

C. 46.7%.

- 2

STUDY SESSION 2 ANSWERS

Reading	Slide Number	Answer
6	39	15.02%
8	97	A

Additional Problems

1. B

2. B

3. C

4. B

Study Session 3

Quantitative Methods: Application

Study Session 3
Quantitative Methods: Application

10. Common Probability Distributions
11. Sampling and Estimation
12. Hypothesis Testing
13. Technical Analysis

KAPLAN SCHOOL OF PROFESSIONAL
UNIVERSITY   AND CONTINUING EDUCATION | **SCHWESER**

© Kaplan, Inc.

Quantitative Methods: Application

10. Common Probability Distributions

KAPLAN SCHOOL OF PROFESSIONAL
UNIVERSITY   AND CONTINUING EDUCATION | **SCHWESER**

LOS 10.a,b Define/Distinguish/Describe
CFAI p. 524, Schweser p. 203

Discrete and Continuous Probability Distributions

A probability distribution gives the probabilities of all possible outcomes for a random variable

A discrete distribution has a finite number of possible outcomes

A continuous distribution has an infinite number of possible outcomes

© Kaplan, Inc.

2

LOS 10.a,b Define/Distinguish/Describe
CFAI p. 524, Schweser p. 203

Probability Functions

- The number of days next week on which it will rain is a discrete random variable that can take on the values {0,1,2,3,4,5,6,7}

- The amount of rain that will fall next week is a continuous random variable

- A probability function, **p(x)**, gives the probability that a discrete random variable will take on the value x

e.g., $p(x) = x / 15$ for $X = \{1,2,3,4,5\}$
→ $p(3) = 20\%$

© Kaplan, Inc.

3

LOS 10.c,d Calculate/Interpret
CFAI p. 526, Schweser p. 205

CDF for a Continuous Distribution

The %ROE, x, for a firm is defined over (−20, +30) and has a CDF of F(x) = (x + 20) / 50. What is the probability that the ROE will be positive and less than or equal to 15?

Prob (0 ≤ x < 15) = F(15) − F(0)

Prob (x ≤ 15) = F(15) = (15 + 20) / 50 = 70%

Prob (x ≤ 0) = F(0) = 20 / 50 = 40%

70 − 40 = 30%

© Kaplan, Inc.

5 - 4

LOS 10.e Define
CFAI p. 526, Schweser p. 206

Binomial Random Variable

The probability of exactly x successes in n trials, given just two possible outcomes (success and failure)

Probability of success on each trial (p) is constant, and trials are independent

$$p(x) = \left(\frac{n!}{(n-x)!\,x!}\right) p^x (1-p)^{n-x}$$

$$= nCx \; p^x (1-p)^{n-x}$$

© Kaplan, Inc.

7

LOS 10.c,d Calculate/Interpret
CFAI p. 526, Schweser p. 205

Cumulative Distribution Function

A cumulative distribution function (cdf), F(x), gives the probability that a random variable will be **less than or equal to** a given value.

For the probability function:
p(x) = x / 15 for X = {1,2,3,4,5}

F(3) = 1 / 15 + 2 / 15 + 3 / 15 = 6 / 15 = 40%

© Kaplan, Inc.

4

LOS 10.e Define
CFAI p. 526, Schweser p. 206

Discrete Uniform

A **discrete uniform distribution** has a finite number of possible outcomes, all of which are equally likely

p(x) = 0.2 for X = {1,2,3,4,5}

p(2) = 20%
F(3) = 60%
Prob(2 ≤ X ≤ 4) = 60%

© Kaplan, Inc.

6

What is the probability of drawing exactly two white marbles from a bowl of white and black marbles in six tries if the probability of selecting white is 0.4 each time?

$x = 2$, $p = 0.4$, $n = 6$

$$p(x) = (nCx)p^x(1-p)^{n-x} = \left(\frac{n!}{(n-x)!x!}\right)p^x(1-p)^{n-x}$$

$$p(2) = 15(0.4)^2(1-0.4)^{6-2} = 0.31$$

© Kaplan, Inc.

8 - 3

Binomial Tree

Two possible outcomes each period, up or down

Prob (up move) + Prob (down move) = 1
Up factor (U) > 1   Down factor (D) = 1/U

Example:
Beginning stock price (S₀) = $20
Prob up = 60% Prob down = 40%
Up factor = 1.12   Down factor 1 / 1.12

© Kaplan, Inc.

9

A Binomial Tree for Stock Price

P(up) = 60%   u = 1.12

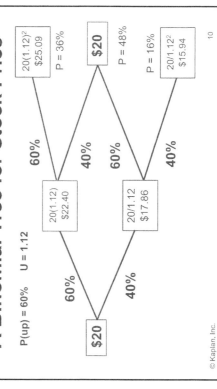

© Kaplan, Inc.

10

Continuous Uniform Distribution

A random variable follows a continuous uniform distribution over the interval 2 to 7.

What is the probability of an outcome between 3 and 6?

$3/5 = 3 \times 20\% = 60\%$

© Kaplan, Inc.

11 - 4

LOS 10.j,k Explain/Distinguish
CFAI p. 541, Schweser p. 212

Common Probability
Distributions

Properties of Normal Distribution

- Completely described by **mean and variance**
- **Symmetric** about the mean (skewness = 0)
- **Kurtosis** (a measure of peakedness) = 3
- Linear combination of normally distributed random variables is also normally distributed
- Probabilities decrease further from the mean, but **the tails go on forever**

Multivariate normal: More than one random variable, need means, variances, and correlation coefficients

© Kaplan, Inc.

12

LOS 10.l Determine
CFAI p. 543, Schweser p. 214

Common Probability
Distributions

Confidence Interval: Normal Distribution

Confidence interval: A range of values around an expected outcome. A random variable is expected to be in this range a certain percentage of the time.

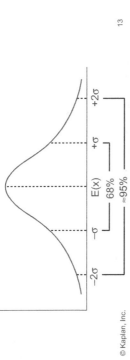

© Kaplan, Inc.

13

LOS 10.l Determine
CFAI p. 543, Schweser p. 214

Common Probability
Distributions

Confidence Intervals: Normal Distribution

68% confidence interval = $\overline{X} \pm 1.00s$

90% confidence interval = $\overline{X} \pm 1.65s$

95% confidence interval = $\overline{X} \pm 1.96s$

99% confidence interval = $\overline{X} \pm 2.58s$

© Kaplan, Inc.

14

Common Probability
Distributions

The mean annual return (normally distributed) on a portfolio over many years is 11%, with a standard deviation of 8%. Calculate a 95% confidence interval on next year's return.

© Kaplan, Inc.

15 - 1

Standard Normal Distribution

- A normal distribution that has been standardized so that **mean = 0 and standard deviation = 1**

- To standardize a random variable, calculate the z-value

- Subtract the mean (so mean = 0) and divide by standard deviation (so σ = 1)

$$z = \frac{X - \mu}{\sigma}$$

> Z is the number of standard deviations from the mean

The EPS for a large group of firms are normally distributed and have **μ = $4.00** and **σ = $1.50**. Find the probability that a randomly selected firm's earnings are less than $3.70.

$$z = \frac{3.70 - 4.00}{1.50} = -0.20$$

Negative Z-table

Z<0	.00	0.01
0.0	0.5000	0.4960
0.1	0.4602	0.4562
0.2	0.4207	0.4168

Standard Normal Probabilities

There is a 42.07% probability that the EPS of a randomly selected firm will be more than 0.20 standard deviations below (above) the mean, < $3.70 (>$4.30).

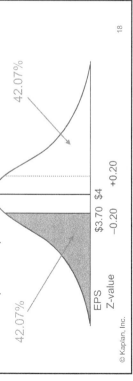

	42.07%	42.07%
EPS	$3.70 $4	
Z-value	−0.20 +0.20	

Shortfall Risk and Safety-First Ratio

<u>Shortfall risk</u>: Probability that a portfolio return or value will be below a target return or value

<u>Roy's Safety-First Ratio</u>: Number of std. dev. target is below the expected return/value

$$SF\ Ratio = \frac{\left[E(R_P) - R_L\right]}{\sigma_P}, \text{ where } R_L = \text{threshold/target return}$$

If R_L = Risk-free rate, SF Ratio is the same as Sharpe ratio

Lognormal Distribution

- If x is normal, e^x is lognormal
- Lognormal is always positive, used for modeling price relatives→ (1 + return) = e^x

Normal Distribution   Lognormal Distribution

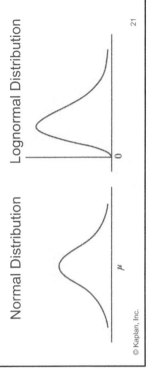

© Kaplan, Inc.

21

Shortfall Risk and Safety-First Ratio

1. Given the two portfolios, which has the lower probability of generating a return below 5%?

	Port. A	Port. B
$E(R_P)$	15%	18%
σ_p	12%	25%
SF Ratio	0.83	0.52
N(–SF Ratio)	0.2033	0.3015

Portfolio A has the larger SF ratio

$$\frac{(15-5)}{12} = 0.83$$

2. Which portfolio has a lower shortfall risk?

Portfolio A has a 20.33% probability of a shortfall

© Kaplan, Inc.

20 - 2

1. If the continuously compounded stated rate = 8%, what is the effective holding period return for one and one-half years?

2. How much will $1,200 grow to in one and one-half years?

© Kaplan, Inc.

23 - 2

Continuous Compounding

Continuously compounded rate = ln(1 + HPR)

EAY with continuous compounding = $e^i - 1$

1. If the 1-year HPR is 8%, what is the continuously compounded rate of return?

$$ln (1.08) = 7.7\%$$

2. If the stated rate is 7.7%, with continuous compounding, what is the EAY?

$$EAY= e^{0.077} - 1 = 8\%$$

© Kaplan, Inc.

22 - 2

Historical Simulation

Similar to Monte Carlo simulation, but values chosen randomly from historical values (not from an assumed distribution)

Advantage: Don't have to estimate distribution of risk factors

Disadvantage: Future outcomes for risk factors may be outside the historical range

25

Quantitative Methods: Application

11. Sampling and Estimation

Monte Carlo Simulation

Simulation can be used to estimate a distribution of derivatives prices or of NPVs

1. Specify distributions of random variables such as interest rates, underlying stock prices

2. Use computer random generation of variables

3. Value the derivative using those values

4. Repeat steps 2 and 3, 1,000s of times

5. Calculate mean/variance of all values

24

Additional Learning Outcomes

LOS 10.h: calculate and interpret tracking error

26

LOS 11.a,b Define/Explain
CFAI p. 576, Schweser p. 240   **Sampling and Estimation**

Sampling

To make inferences about the parameters of a population, we will use a **sample** from the population

A **simple random sample** is one where every population member has an equal chance of being selected

A **sampling distribution** is the distribution of sample statistics for repeated samples of size n

Sampling error is the difference between a sample statistic and true population parameter (e.g., $\bar{x} - \mu$)

© Kaplan, Inc.   28

LOS 11.c Distinguish
CFAI p. 577, Schweser p. 241   **Sampling and Estimation**

Stratified Random Sampling

1. **Create subgroups** from population based on important characteristics (e.g., identify bonds according to callable, ratings, maturity, coupon)

2. **Select samples** from each subgroup in proportion to the size of the subgroup

Used to:
- Construct a sample that matches the underlying population in certain characteristics
- Construct bond portfolios to track a bond index

© Kaplan, Inc.   29

LOS 11.e Explain
CFAI p. 582, Schweser p. 242   **Sampling and Estimation**

Central Limit Theorem

For any population with mean μ and variance σ^2, as the size of a random sample gets large, the distribution of sample means approaches a normal distribution with **mean μ and variance σ^2/n**

Allows us to make inferences about and construct **confidence intervals** for population means based on sample means

© Kaplan, Inc.   30

LOS 11.f Calculate/Interpret
CFAI p. 582, Schweser p. 243   **Sampling and Estimation**

Standard Error of the Sample Mean

Standard error of sample mean is the <u>standard deviation</u> of the **distribution of sample means** for samples of size n.

$$\sigma_{\bar{x}} = \frac{\sigma}{\sqrt{n}} \text{ or } S_{\bar{x}} = \frac{s}{\sqrt{n}}$$

© Kaplan, Inc.   31

Desirable Estimator Properties

1. Unbiased – expected value equal to parameter

2. Efficient – sampling distribution has smallest variance of all unbiased estimators

3. Consistent – larger sample → better estimator
   Standard error of estimate decreases with larger sample size

© Kaplan, Inc.   33

The mean P/E for a sample of 41 firms is 19.0 and the standard deviation of the population is 6.6. What is the standard error of the *sample mean?*

$$\sigma_{\bar{x}} = \frac{\sigma}{\sqrt{n}} = \frac{6.6}{\sqrt{41}} = 1.03$$

For samples of size n = 41, the distribution of the **sample means** has a mean of 19.0 and a standard deviation of 1.03.

© Kaplan, Inc.   32 - 2

Student's *t*-Distribution and Degrees of Freedom

Properties of Student's *t*-Distribution

- Symmetrical (bell shaped)
- Fatter tails than a normal distribution
- Defined by single parameter, degrees of freedom (df), where df = n – 1
- As df increase, *t*-distribution approaches normal distribution

© Kaplan, Inc.   35

The mean P/E for a sample of 41 firms is 19.0. The population is approximately normal and the std dev of the population is 6.6. Calculate:

1. 90% confidence interval for the mean

2. 95% confidence interval for the mean

3. 95% confidence interval for P/E of a random firm

© Kaplan, Inc.   34 - 3

LOS 11.i Describe/Calculate/Interpret
CFAI p. 590, Schweser p. 245   Sampling and Estimation

t-Distribution

The figure below shows the shape of the
t-distribution with different degrees of freedom.

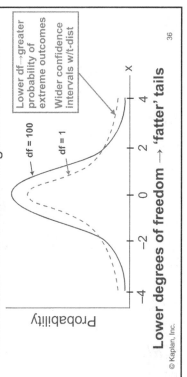

Lower df → greater
probability of
extreme outcomes

Wider confidence
intervals w/t-dist

df = 100

df = 1

Probability

x

Lower degrees of freedom → 'fatter' tails

© Kaplan, Inc.

36

LOS 11.j Calculate/Interpret
CFAI p. 587, Schweser p. 247   Sampling and Estimation

Confidence Intervals for Mean

| When sampling from a: | | Reliability Factors | |
Distribution	Variance	Small Sample (n < 30)	Large Sample (n > 30)
Normal	Known	z-statistic	z-statistic
Normal	Unknown	t-statistic	t-statistic*
Nonnormal	Known	Not available	z-statistic
Nonnormal	Unknown	Not available	t-statistic*

*The z-statistic is theoretically acceptable

© Kaplan, Inc.

37

LOS 11.j Calculate/Interpret
CFAI p. 587, Schweser p. 247   Sampling and Estimation

Confidence Interval for Mean

The sample mean is 19.0, the <u>sample standard
deviation</u> is 6.6, and n = 41. Establish a 90%
confidence interval for the population mean.

standard error of mean $= \dfrac{s}{\sqrt{n}} = \dfrac{6.6}{\sqrt{41}} = 1.03$

From t-table, reliability factor is 1.684 (df = 40, a/2 = 0.05)

degrees of freedom ⟋   ↖ 5% in each tail

$19.0 \pm 1.684\,(1.03) = 17.27 < \text{mean} < 20.73$

© Kaplan, Inc.

38 - 3

LOS 11.k Describe
CFAI p. 595, Schweser p. 252   Sampling and Estimation

Sample Size Issues

We've seen that larger samples produce better
estimates and smaller confidence intervals, **but:**

Cost can be a factor—obtaining more data can
increase costs, so there is a trade-off

Including more data points from a population
(time period) with *different parameters* will not
improve your estimate

© Kaplan, Inc.

39

LOS 11.k Describe
CFAI p. 595, Schweser p. 252   **Sampling and Estimation**

Types of Bias

Data-mining bias – from repeatedly doing tests on same data sample

Sample selection bias – sample not really random

Survivorship bias – sampling only surviving firms, mutual funds, hedge funds

Look-ahead bias – using information not available at the time to construct sample

Time-period bias – relationship exists only during the time period of sample data

© Kaplan, Inc.   40

Additional Learning Outcomes

LOS 11.d: time series, cross-sectional data

© Kaplan, Inc.   41

Quantitative Methods: Application

12. Hypothesis Testing

KAPLAN SCHOOL OF PROFESSIONAL
UNIVERSITY AND CONTINUING EDUCATION | **SCHWESER**

LOS 12.a Define/Describe/Interpret
CFAI p. 617, Schweser p. 264

Steps in Hypothesis Testing

1. State the hypothesis—relation to be tested
2. Select a test statistic
3. Specify the level of significance
4. State the decision rule for the hypothesis
5. Collect the sample and calculate statistics
6. Make a decision about the hypothesis
7. Make a decision based on the test results

© Kaplan, Inc.   43

LOS 12.a Define/Describe/Interpret
CFAI p. 617, Schweser p. 264   Hypothesis Testing

Null and Alternative Hypotheses

Null hypothesis (H$_0$)
1. The hypothesis to be tested
2. Researcher typically wants to reject it
3. Always <u>includes the equal sign</u>

Alternative hypothesis (H$_a$)
Supported if the researcher rejects the null hypothesis

© Kaplan, Inc.   44

LOS 12.c Explain
CFAI p. 619, Schweser p. 269   Hypothesis Testing

Test Statistic and Critical Values

- A test statistic is (1) calculated from sample data and (2) compared to critical value(s) to test H$_0$

- If the test statistic exceeds the critical value (or is outside the range of critical values), the researcher rejects H$_0$

  - Critical values are like a confidence interval

© Kaplan, Inc.   45

LOS 12.b Distinguish
CFAI p. 618, Schweser p. 265   Hypothesis Testing

Two-Tailed Test

Use when testing to see if a population parameter is different from a specified value

H$_0$: $\mu = 0$ versus H$_a$: $\mu \neq 0$

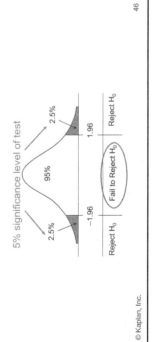

© Kaplan, Inc.   46

LOS 12.b Distinguish
CFAI p. 618, Schweser p. 265   Hypothesis Testing

One-Tailed Test

Use when testing to see if a parameter is <u>above</u> or <u>below</u> a specified value

H$_0$: $\mu \leq 0$ versus H$_a$: $\mu > 0$
H$_0$: $\mu \geq 0$ versus H$_a$: $\mu < 0$

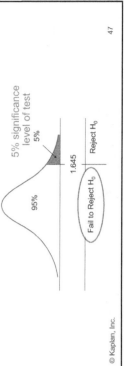

© Kaplan, Inc.   47

Type I and Type II Errors

Type I Error: Rejecting H_0 when it is actually true

Type II Error: Failing to reject H_0 when it is false

Significance level is Probability of Type I Error

[e.g., convicting an innocent person (null is innocent)]

Power of test is 1 – Prob. of Type II Error

(e.g., failing to convict a guilty person)

© Kaplan, Inc.   48

Statistically vs.
Economically Meaningful Result

Statistical significance does not necessarily imply **economic significance**:

Transactions costs

Taxes

Risk

© Kaplan, Inc.   49

p-value Example

A *p*-value is the smallest level of significance at which the null can be rejected, the probability of getting the test statistic by chance if the null is true.

If the *p*-value is given as 0.0213 or 2.13%:

We **can** reject the null at 5% significance.

We **can** reject the null at 3% significance.

We **cannot** reject the null at 1% significance.

© Kaplan, Inc.   50

Data for a fund:

Sample mean = 1.5%   Sample size = 45

Population std dev = 1.4%   Population non-normal

Can we reject the hypothesis that a fund's mean return is **equal to** 1% per month, at the 95% level?

© Kaplan, Inc.   51-3

Test Statistics

LOS: Identify the appropriate test statistic and interpret the results…

Difference in means test: Numerator is the difference between sample means of two independent normal populations
t-test, reject if test statistic is outside critical values

Mean differences (paired comparison) test: Numerator is the mean difference between paired observations from two dependent normal populations
t-test, reject if test statistic is outside critical values

© Kaplan, Inc.   53

Parametric and Nonparametric Tests

Parametric tests are based on assumptions about population distributions and population parameters (e.g., t-test, z-test, F-test)

Nonparametric tests make few if any assumptions about the population distribution and test things other than parameter values (e.g., runs tests, rank correlation tests)

© Kaplan, Inc.   55

Hypothesis Testing

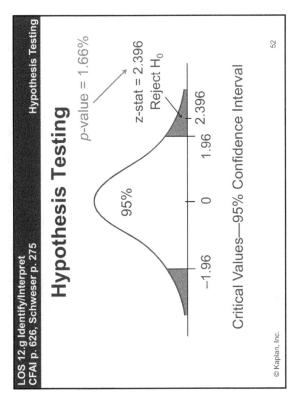

p-value = 1.66%

z-stat = 2.396

Reject H$_0$

95%

−1.96   0   1.96   2.396

Critical Values—95% Confidence Interval

© Kaplan, Inc.   52

Other Tests

Test of whether the variance of a normal population equals σ_0^2 uses a **Chi-square** test statistic, two-tailed test, reject if outside the critical values

Test of whether the variances of two normal populations are equal is an **F-test**

Putting the larger sample variance in the numerator allows us to **consider only upper critical value** – although F-test is a two-tailed test

© Kaplan, Inc.   54

Quantitative Methods: Application

13. Technical Analysis

Technical Analysis

LOS 13.a Explain
CFAI p. 670, Schweser p. 304

Principles and Assumptions of Technical Analysis

- Stock values determined by supply and demand which are **driven by both rational and irrational behavior**

  - Technical analysts use prices and trading volume to analyze changes in supply and demand

  - Security **prices move in trends** that persist for long periods and repeat themselves in predictable ways

57

Technical Analysis

LOS 13.a Explain
CFAI p. 670, Schweser p. 304

Technical Analysis vs. Fundamental Analysis

Fundamental analysts look for changes in intrinsic values (what prices **should** be) based primarily on anticipated financial results and estimates of future cash flows

Technical analysts try to predict price change though analysis of past trading prices and volume

58

Technical Analysis

LOS 13.a Explain
CFAI p. 670, Schweser p. 304

Claimed Advantages of Technical Analysis

- It is based on actual trade data, whereas fundamental analysis is based on accounting numbers which can be estimates

  - Can be used for assets with **no cash flows** to discount for valuation (e.g., commodities)

  - Don't have to learn accounting!

    LOS b, c, d, e, f, g, and h are left for self-study

59

Quantitative Methods

Additional Problems

KAPLAN UNIVERSITY SCHOOL OF PROFESSIONAL AND CONTINUING EDUCATION | SCHWESER

Technical Analysis

Additional Study

LOS 13.b: technical analysis charts

LOS 13.c: trend, support, resistance

LOS 13.d: chart patterns

LOS 13.e: technical analysis indicators

LOS 13.f: cycles

LOS 13.g: Elliott wave theory

LOS 13.h: intermarket analysis

© Kaplan, Inc.

60

Additional Problems

2) Free cash flow per share for a population of companies is approximately normal, has a mean of $2.50, and a standard deviation of $0.50. The probability that a firm chosen at random will have cash flow per share of less than $2.00 is:

A. 16%.

B. 50%.

C. 84%.

© Kaplan, Inc.

-1-

Additional Problems

1) Returns on an index of 100 stocks are approximately normal, have a mean of 9% and std. dev. of 15%. A 99% confidence interval on next year's index return is:

A. −20.4% to 38.4%.

B. −29.7% to 47.7%.

C. 5.1% to 12.9%.

© Kaplan, Inc.

-3-

Additional Problems

4) A sample of 9 high-yield bond returns was taken from a normally distributed population. The population has a mean of 16% and a variance of 144. If a bond from the population is randomly selected, a 90% confidence interval for its return is:

A. −3.74% to 35.74%.

B. 0.64% to 31.36%.

C. 11.26% to 16.74%.

- 4

Additional Problems

6) Quarterly returns on an index are approximately normally distributed with a standard deviation of 10%. Index returns over the most recent 20 quarters have a mean of 4%. Should a researcher who wants to show that the average quarterly returns for this index are positive reject the null hypothesis at the 5% significance level?

- 3

Additional Problems

3) A sample of 64 high-yield bond returns was taken from a normally distributed population. The sample mean was 14%, and the sample standard deviation was 25%. The 95% confidence interval in which the population mean lies is *closest* to:

A. 13% to 15%.

B. 11% to 17%.

C. 8% to 20%.

- 4

CFA Curriculum Vol. 1, R.12, Q.18, p. 659

5) All else equal, is specifying a smaller significance level in a hypothesis test likely to increase the probability of a:

	Type I error?	Type II error?
A.	No	No
B.	No	Yes
C.	Yes	Yes

- 3

Additional Problems

8) The continuously compounded rate of return on an investment is 4.4%. Its effective annual return is *closest* to:

A. 4.45%.

B. 4.50%.

C. 4.55%.

Additional Problems

7) The probability that a stock's return will be greater than the return on an index in any given week is 60%. The probability that the stock's return will be greater than the return on the index in 31 weeks out of the 52 weeks next year is *closest* to:

A. 11%.

B. 13%.

C. 15%.

Reading	Slide Number	Answer
10	15	−4.7% to 26.7%
10	23(1)	12.75%
10	23(2)	$1,353
11	34(1)	17.3 < mean < 20.7
11	34(2)	17.0 < mean < 21.0
11	34(3)	6.06 < P/E < 31.94
12	51	z-stat = 2.396; reject

Additional Problems

1. B

2. A

3. C

4. A

5. B

6. z-stat = 1.789; reject

7. A

8. B

Study Session 4

Economics: Microeconomics and Macroeconomics

Slide 1:

Economics

Microeconomics and Macroeconomics

14. Topics in Demand and Supply Analysis

KAPLAN UNIVERSITY | SCHOOL OF PROFESSIONAL AND CONTINUING EDUCATION | SCHWESER

Slide 2:

Economics

Study Session 4
Microeconomics and Macroeconomics

14. Topics in Demand and Supply Analysis
15. The Firm and Market Structures
16. Aggregate Output, Prices, and Economic Growth
17. Understanding Business Cycles

KAPLAN UNIVERSITY | SCHOOL OF PROFESSIONAL AND CONTINUING EDUCATION | SCHWESER

Slide 3:

LOS 14.a Calculate/Interpret/Describe
CFAI p. 9, Schweser p. 1

Topics in Demand and Supply Analysis

Factors That Influence Elasticity of Demand

- Availability and closeness of **substitutes**

  ↑ Substitutes: ↑ Elasticity

- **Proportion of income** spent on the item

  ↑ Proportion of income: ↑ Elasticity

- **Time** elapsed since previous price change

  ↑ Time: ↑ Elasticity

© Kaplan, Inc.

3 - 3

Slide 4:

LOS 14.a Calculate/Interpret/Describe
CFAI p. 9, Schweser p. 1

Topics in Demand and Supply Analysis

Price Elasticity of Demand

Price Elasticity of Demand (PED) $= \dfrac{\%\Delta Q_X}{\%\Delta P_X}$

As the price of a normal good increases, **quantity demanded** decreases

Elastic demand: Percentage increase in price leads to a larger percentage decrease in quantity demanded

Inelastic demand: Percentage increase in price leads to a smaller percentage decrease in quantity demanded

© Kaplan, Inc.

2

Price Elasticity of Demand

Elastic

Price

D

Quantity

Inelastic

Price

D

Quantity

Perfectly Inelastic/Elastic

Price

$D_{Perfectly\ Inelastic}$

$D_{Perfectly\ Elastic}$

Quantity

© Kaplan, Inc.

4

Elasticity on a Straight-line Demand Curve

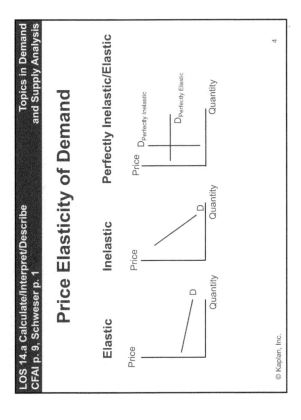

Price

8
7
6
5
4
3
2
1

(a) high elasticity

(b) unitary elasticity
elasticity = −1

(c) low elasticity

10 20 30 40 50 60 70 80   Quantity

Slope of demand curve ≠ price elasticity

Slope depends on units price and quantity are measured in. Elasticity is based on % change

© Kaplan, Inc.

5

Calculating Elasticity at a Point

Price elasticity of demand (PED) = $\dfrac{\%\Delta Q_X}{\%\Delta P_X}$

$$\frac{\%\Delta Q_X}{\%\Delta P_X} = \frac{\Delta Q_X/Q_0}{\Delta P_X/P_0} = \frac{P_0}{Q_0} \times \frac{\Delta Q_X}{\Delta P_X}$$

Slope coefficient of price (−140)

Calculate PED at a price of €150:

$Q_{DX} = 29,500 − 140\ P_X$

$Q_{DX} = 29,500 − (140 \times 150)$

$Q_{DX} = 8,500$

$$PED = \left(\frac{150}{8,500}\right) \times (-140) = -2.47$$

© Kaplan, Inc.

6 - 2

The market demand function for four-year private universities is given by the equation

$Qd = 84 − 3.1P_{private} + 0.8Income + 0.9P_{public}.$

Assume that $P_{private}$ = 38, Income = 100, and P_{public} is equal to 18.

The price elasticity of demand for private universities is *closest* to:

A. −3.1.

B. −1.9.

C. 0.6.

© Kaplan, Inc.

7 - 2

Cross Price Elasticity of Demand

Price of coffee increased 16.65% and demand for tea increased 11.10%.

$$\text{cross price elasticity of demand} = \frac{11.10\%}{16.65\%} = 0.67$$

cross price elasticity > 0: the goods are *substitutes*

Price of pizza increased 25.0% and demand for cola decreased 10.7%.

$$\text{cross price elasticity of demand} = \frac{-10.7\%}{25.0\%} = -0.43$$

cross price elasticity < 0: the goods are *complements*

© Kaplan, Inc.   8

Income Elasticity of Demand

The sensitivity of quantity demanded to changes in income

$$\text{income elasticity} = \frac{\%\ \text{change in quantity demanded}}{\%\ \text{change in income}}$$

Normal good: Income↑ Demand↑ Inc. Elasticity > 0

Inferior good: Income↑ Demand↓ Elasticity < 0
(e.g., bus travel)

© Kaplan, Inc.   9

Substitution and Income Effects

When the price of a good falls, consumers purchase more of that good and less of other goods. **(substitution effect)**

A decrease in the price of a good that a consumer purchases results in extra income if purchases remain the same. **(income effect)**

This 'increase' in income will:

Increase consumption of the good if it is *normal*.

Decrease consumption of the good if it is *inferior*.

© Kaplan, Inc.   10

Substitution and Income Effects

Normal good: Income and substitution effects of a price decrease on purchases are both positive

Inferior good: Substitution effect of a price decrease is positive, but the income effect is negative

Giffen good: An inferior good for which the negative income effect of a price decrease outweighs the positive substitution effect
Demand curve could slope upward for some.

© Kaplan, Inc.   11

CFA Curriculum Vol. 2,
R.14, Q.7, p. 52

In the case of a normal good with a decrease in own price, which of the following statements is *most likely* true?

A. Both the substitution and income effects lead to an increase in the quantity purchased.

B. The substitution effect leads to an increase in the quantity purchased, while the income effect has no impact.

C. The substitution effect leads to an increase in the quantity purchased, while the income effect leads to a decrease.

12 – 1

LOS 14.d Describe
CFAI p. 23, Schweser p. 9

Total, Marginal, and Average Product of Labor

Workers	Total Product	Marginal Product	Average Product
1	8	8	8
2	20	12	10
3	26	6	8.7
4	30	4	7.5
5	32	2	6.4
6	33	1	5.5

$33 \div 6 = 5.5$

© Kaplan, Inc.

13

LOS 14.d Describe
CFAI p. 23, Schweser p. 9

Diminishing Marginal Returns

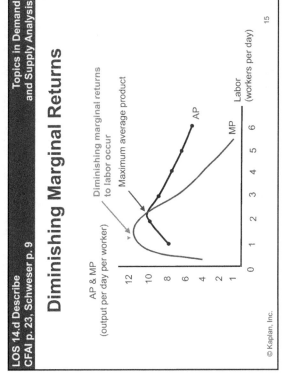

Marginal product, holding other inputs constant, first increases and then decreases

Marginal product (output per worker–day)

Diminishing marginal returns to labor occur

MP

Workers per day

© Kaplan, Inc.

14

LOS 14.d Describe
CFAI p. 23, Schweser p. 9

Diminishing Marginal Returns

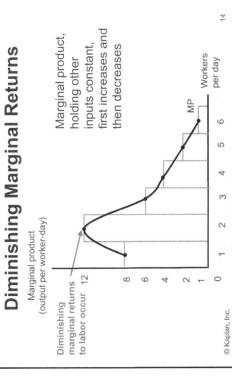

AP & MP
(output per day per worker)

Diminishing marginal returns to labor occur

Maximum average product

AP

MP

Labor (workers per day)

© Kaplan, Inc.

15

Costs per Unit of Output

Average costs and marginal costs

$$ATC = AFC + AVC$$

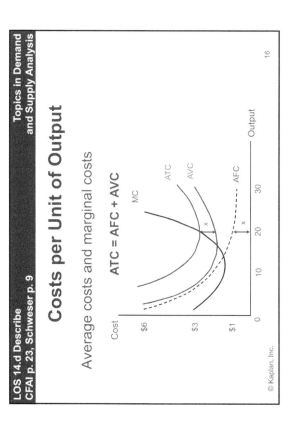

16

Breakeven and Shutdown

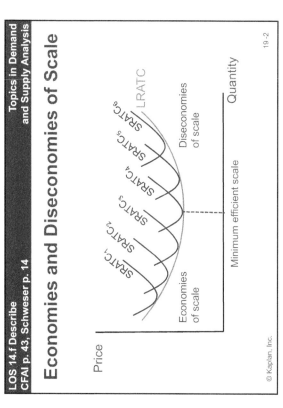

17 - 2

The short-term shutdown point of production for a firm operating under perfect competition will *most likely* occur when:
A. price is equal to average total cost.
B. marginal revenue is equal to marginal cost.
C. marginal revenue is less than average variable costs.

18 - 1

Economies and Diseconomies of Scale

19 -2

Slide 21

Characteristics of Market Structures

	Perfect Competition	Monopolistic Competition	Oligopoly	Monopoly
Number of sellers	Many firms	Many firms	Few firms	Single firm
Barriers to entry	Very low	Low	High	Very high
Nature of substitute products	Very good substitutes	Good substitutes but differentiated	Very good substitutes or differentiated	No good substitutes
Nature of competition	Price only	Price, marketing, features	Price, marketing, features	Advertising
Price power	None	Some	Some to significant	Significant

© Kaplan, Inc.   21

Slide (title)

Economics

Microeconomics and Macroeconomics

15. The Firm and Market Structures

KAPLAN UNIVERSITY — SCHOOL OF PROFESSIONAL AND CONTINUING EDUCATION | SCHWESER

Slide 22

Perfect Competition

Firms in perfect competition are **price takers**
- No influence over market price
- "Take" the equilibrium (market) price as given

Market Characteristics:
- Homogeneous product
- Large number of independent firms; each small relative to the total market
- No barriers to entry or exit
- Supply and demand determine market price

© Kaplan, Inc.   22

Slide 23

Perfect Competition – LR Equilibrium

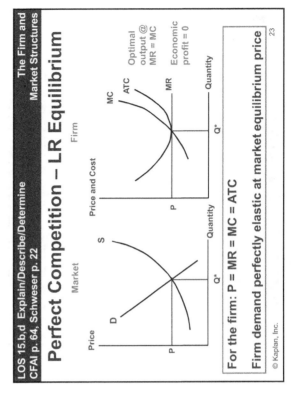

Optimal output @ MR = MC

Economic profit = 0

For the firm: P = MR = MC = ATC

Firm demand perfectly elastic at market equilibrium price

© Kaplan, Inc.   23

Perfect Competition

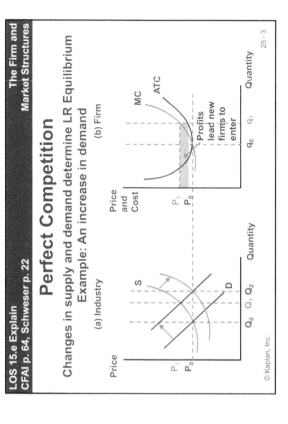

(a) Firm Supply

(b) Market Supply

P < AVC:	**AVC ≤ P < ATC:**	**Price > ATC:**
Insufficient to cover fixed or variable cost	Insufficient to cover fixed costs; variable costs covered	All costs covered, positive profit

© Kaplan, Inc.

24 - 3

Perfect Competition

Changes in supply and demand determine LR Equilibrium
Example: An increase in demand

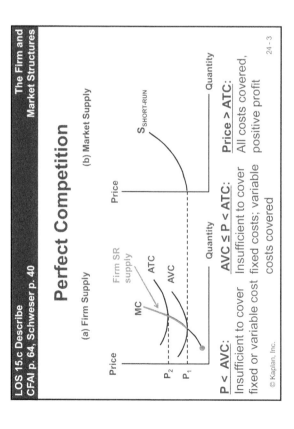

(a) Industry

(b) Firm

Profits lead new firms to enter

© Kaplan, Inc.

25 - 3

Pure Monopoly

Single producer of a product with no good substitutes

<u>Barriers to entry:</u>

- Economies of scale (natural monopoly)
- Government licensing and legal barriers
- Resource control

A **single-price monopolist** must reduce price to sell more; thus, **marginal revenue is less than price**

With price discrimination, buyers charged different prices (can increase economic efficiency)

© Kaplan, Inc.

27

For Acme Corp., the market price of their product permanently falls below ATC but is above AVC and MC. In the short run and long run, Acme should:

	Short Run	Long Run
A.	shut down	shut down
B.	shut down	operate
C.	operate	shut down

© Kaplan, Inc.

26 - 1

LOS 15.b Explain
CFAI p. 64, Schweser p. 22

The Firm and
Market Structures

Marginal and Average Revenue

| Total Revenue = P × Q |
| Marginal Revenue = ΔTR / ΔQ |
| Average Revenue = TR / Q = Price |

Price

P_M

Perfectly
Elastic
Demand

Market Price = MR = AR

Quantity

© Kaplan, Inc.

28

LOS 15.b Explain
CFAI p. 64, Schweser p. 22

The Firm and
Market Structures

Marginal and Average Revenue

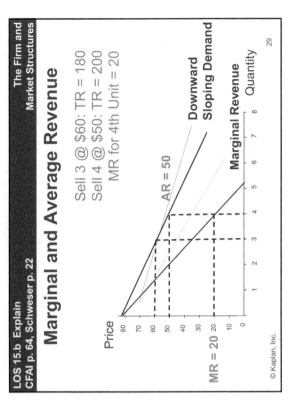

Sell 3 @ $60: TR = 180
Sell 4 @ $50: TR = 200
MR for 4th Unit = 20

Price

AR = 50

MR = 20

Downward
Sloping Demand

Marginal Revenue

Quantity

© Kaplan, Inc.

29

LOS 15.b,c,d Explain, Describe/Determine
CFAI p. 64, Schweser p. 22

The Firm and
Market Structures

Pure Monopoly

Maximize profit at MC = MR
P > ATC, Econ profit > 0

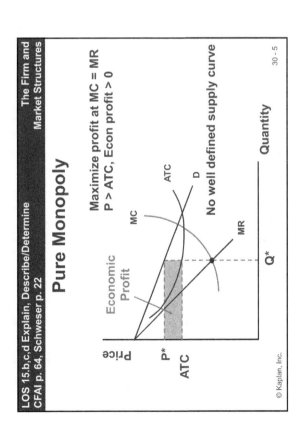

Price

P*
ATC

Economic
Profit

MC

ATC

D

MR

Q*

No well defined supply curve

Quantity

© Kaplan, Inc.

30 - 5

LOS 15.e Explain
CFAI p. 64, Schweser p. 22

The Firm and
Market Structures

Pure Monopoly

Long-run Equilibrium

If unregulated, the firm must defend monopoly position to continue to earn economic profits

If regulated, regulators may attempt to **set price:**

  = ATC so that output and consumer surplus increase, and economic profit is zero

  = MC to maximize surplus, but if MC < ATC, will require a subsidy to operate

In theory, regulated monopoly with large economies of scale could be economically efficient

© Kaplan, Inc.

31

Monopolistic Competition

- A large number of firms in industry:
  - Each firm has a small market share
  - Concerned about average price
  - Collusion not possible
- Firms produce <u>differentiated products</u> (close but not perfect substitutes)
- <u>Relatively elastic demand</u>
- Firms compete on <u>price, quality, and marketing</u>
- Low barriers to entry

© Kaplan, Inc.

32

Monopolistic Competition

SR equilibrium output

Relations of P, MR, MC
same as monopoly

LR firm equilibrium

No well-defined supply function

P = ATC with low cost entry

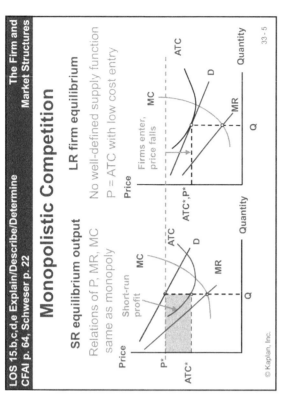

© Kaplan, Inc.

33 - 5

Monopolistic Competition

In the long run:

- With low entry costs, LR economic profit = 0
- Firms spend on marketing and product differentiation
- Each firm still produces at MR = MC quantity
- Output is less than with perfect competition
- However, differentiation, advertising, and brand names may have economic value to consumers

© Kaplan, Inc.

34

Oligopoly

- **Small number** of sellers – downward sloping firm demand curves
- Firms' demand curves less elastic than monopolistic competition
- **Interdependence** among competitors and their demand curves
- Significant **barriers to entry** (e.g., scale of operations)
- Products may be similar *or* differentiated

© Kaplan, Inc.

35

Oligopoly Pricing Models

Dominant firm (low cost, large market share) model

Dominant firm **essentially sets market price**

Other firms choose output that maximizes profit
(MC = MR) at the price established by the dominant firm

© Kaplan, Inc.

37

Oligopoly Pricing Models

Cournot Duopoly assumptions:

- Two firms have identical marginal costs
- Homogeneous product
- Firms have market power

Results:

- Each firm ends up supplying half the market
- Price is less than with collusion, but greater than with perfect competition
- Quantity is greater than with collusion, but less than with perfect competition

© Kaplan, Inc.

39

Oligopoly Pricing Models

With **collusion**, P, MC, MR, ATC relations are same as monopoly—each firm restricts output and firms share the **economic profit**

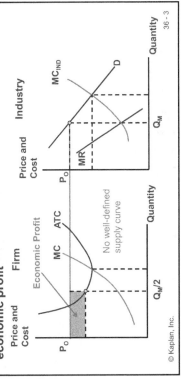

© Kaplan, Inc.

36 - 3

Oligopoly Pricing Models

Kinked Demand Curve Model

- Competitors **will not** follow a price increase
- Competitors **will** follow a price decrease
- Model gives a discontinuous marginal revenue curve (gap)
- Model does not specify what determines the market price P_K

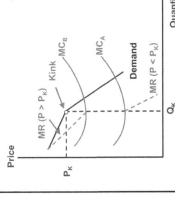

© Kaplan, Inc.

38 - 3

Oligopoly and Game Theory

Oligopoly firms can earn a greater profit if they **collude**, fix industry output at the monopoly (profit maximizing) quantity, and share the profits

Game theory suggests that if competitors cannot detect cheating, they will choose to violate the collusion agreement and increase output

© Kaplan, Inc.

40

Oligopoly and Game Theory

Nash Equilibrium: Choices of all firms are such that no other choice makes any firm better off (increases profits or decreases losses)

Strategic games model the best choice for a firm depending on the actions and reactions of competitors

© Kaplan, Inc.

41

Nash Equilibrium and Oligopoly

	Firm B honors	Firm B cheats
Firm A honors	A profit = $225m B profit = $225m	A profit = $75m B profit = $300m
Firm A cheats	A profit = $300m B profit = $75m	A profit = $150m B profit = $150m

Nash Equilibrium

Collusion will be more successful with:

- Fewer firms
- Homogeneous products
- Similar cost structures
- Certain and severe retaliation for cheating
- Little competition from firms outside the agreement

© Kaplan, Inc.

42 – 3

Pricing Strategy Summary

- **Perfect Competition:** Price = MR = MC at profit maximizing output quantity
- **Monopoly, Monopolistic Competition:** MR = MC at profit maximizing output quantity; price determined by downward-sloping demand curve; P > MR
- **Oligopoly:** Optimal pricing strategy depends on how other firms are expected to react
  - Cournot Duopoly
  - Kinked demand curve
  - Dominant firm
  - Game theory, Collusion

© Kaplan, Inc.

43

Concentration Measures

N-Firm Concentration Ratio: Sum of the percentage market shares of the *N* largest firms in an industry

Advantage: Simple

Limitations: Ignores barriers to entry, largely unaffected by mergers

Herfindahl-Hirschman Index (HHI): Sum of <u>squared</u> market shares of *N* largest firms in a market

Advantages: More sensitive to mergers than *N*-firm ratio, widely used by regulators

Limitations: Ignores barriers to entry, ignores elasticity of demand

© Kaplan, Inc.

44

A market where individual producers face downward sloping demand, barriers to entry are low, and producer pricing decisions are not directly affected by decisions of other producers is referred to as:

A. an oligopoly.

B. perfect competition.

C. monopolistic competition.

© Kaplan, Inc.

45 - 1

Microeconomics and Macroeconomics

16. Aggregate Output, Prices, and Economic Growth

Gross Domestic Product (GDP)

Market value of all final goods and services produced in a country/economy

- Produced during the period

- Only goods that are valued in the market

- Final goods and services only (not intermediate)

- Rental value for owner-occupied housing (estimated)

- Government services (at cost)—not transfers

© Kaplan, Inc.

47

LOS 16.a Calculate/Explain
CFAI p. 116, Schweser p. 52

Aggregate Output, Prices,
and Economic Growth

Calculating GDP
Income Approach

Income of households + businesses + government

Expenditures Approach

Sum the market values of all final goods and services produced in the economy

OR

Sum all the increases in value at each stage of the production process

© Kaplan, Inc.

48

LOS 16.a Calculate/Explain
CFAI p. 116, Schweser p. 52

Aggregate Output, Prices,
and Economic Growth

GDP: Expenditures Approach
GDP = C + I + G + (X − M)

C = consumption spending

I = business investment (capital equipment + change in inventories)

G = government purchases

X = exports

M = imports

© Kaplan, Inc.

49

LOS 16.c Compare/Calculate/Interpret
CFAI p. 120, Schweser p. 53

Aggregate Output, Prices,
and Economic Growth

Nominal vs. Real GDP

Nominal GDP

Sum of all current-year goods and services at current-year prices.

$$\sum Q_t \times P_t$$

Real GDP (measures increase in physical output)

Sum of all current year goods and services at base-year prices.

With base year = t − 5:

$$\sum Q_t \times P_{t-5}$$

© Kaplan, Inc.

50

LOS 16.c Compare/Calculate/Interpret
CFAI p. 120, Schweser p. 53

Aggregate Output, Prices,
and Economic Growth

GDP Deflator

$$GDP\ Deflator = \frac{Nominal\ GDP}{Real\ GDP} \times 100$$

With base year t − 5, a GDP deflator of 112.3 means prices have gone up by 12.3% over 5 years—a measure of inflation.

$$Real\ GDP = \frac{Nominal\ GDP}{GDP\ Deflator} \times 100 = \frac{Nominal\ GDP}{\left(\dfrac{GDP\ Deflator}{100}\right)}$$

© Kaplan, Inc.

51

Aggregate Output, Prices,
and Economic Growth

National Income

GDP = **national income**

+ capital consumption allowance

+ statistical discrepancy

Capital consumption allowance is the output that goes to replace capital stock wearing out, depreciation

© Kaplan, Inc.

52

Aggregate Output, Prices,
and Economic Growth

National Income

National income =

employees' wages and benefits

+ corporate and government profits <u>pre-tax</u>

+ interest income

+ unincorporated business owners' income

+ rent

+ indirect business taxes – subsidies

(taxes and subsidies included in final prices)

© Kaplan, Inc.

53

Aggregate Output, Prices,
and Economic Growth

Personal Income

Personal income =

national income

+ transfer payments to households

– indirect business taxes

– corporate income taxes

– undistributed corporate profits

© Kaplan, Inc.

54

Aggregate Output, Prices,
and Economic Growth

Personal Disposable Income

Personal disposable income =

personal income – personal taxes =

after-tax income

Each period, individuals decide whether to consume or save disposable income.

© Kaplan, Inc.

55

Aggregate Output, Prices, and Economic Growth

In the income-based approach to calculating gross domestic product, the difference between national income and gross domestic product is:

A. depreciation.

B. corporate income taxes.

C. transfer payments from government to individuals.

Aggregate Output, Prices, and Economic Growth

The GDP deflator is calculated as 100 times:

A. $\dfrac{\text{current year nominal GDP}}{\text{base year nominal GDP}}$

B. $\dfrac{\text{base year output at current year prices}}{\text{base year nominal GDP}}$

C. $\dfrac{\text{current year nominal GDP}}{\text{current year output at base year prices}}$

LOS 16.e Explain
CFAI p. 133, Schweser p. 56

Aggregate Output, Prices, and Economic Growth

Deriving the Fundamental Relationship

GDP = C + I + G + (X − M)   Total Expenditures

GDP = C + S + T   Total Income

$$\cancel{C} + S + T = \cancel{C} + I + G + (X - M)$$

$$S + T = I + G + (X - M)$$

$$S = I + (G - T) + (X - M)$$

LOS 16.e Explain
CFAI p. 133, Schweser p. 56

Aggregate Output, Prices, and Economic Growth

Fundamental Relationship

$$S = I + (G - T) + (X - M)$$

Savings = Investment + Fiscal Balance + Trade Balance

Savings are either invested, used to finance government deficit, or used to fund a trade surplus, when both exist.

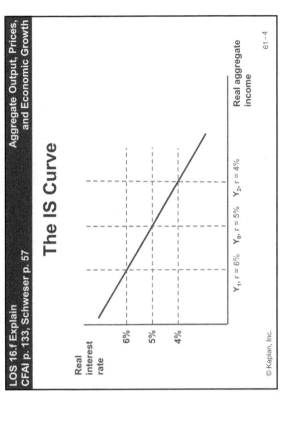

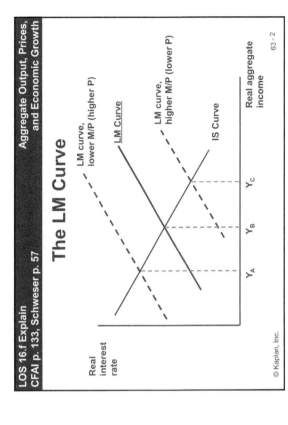

LOS 16.f Explain
CFAI p. 133, Schweser p. 57

Aggregate Output, Prices, and Economic Growth

The Aggregate Demand Curve

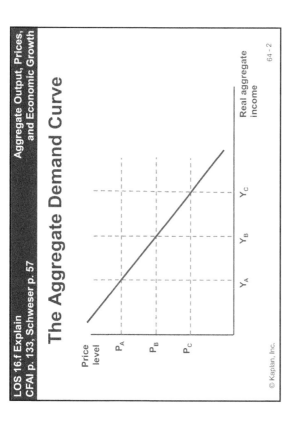

64 - 2

CFA Curriculum Vol. 2,
R.16, Q.17, p. 188

Aggregate Output, Prices, and Economic Growth

An increase in the nominal money supply would shift the:

A. IS curve and the LM curve.

B. IS curve and the aggregate demand curve.

C. LM curve and the aggregate demand curve.

65 - 1

CFA Curriculum Vol. 2,
R.16, Q.18, p. 188

Aggregate Output, Prices, and Economic Growth

An increase in the price level would shift the:

A. IS curve.

B. LM curve.

C. aggregate demand curve.

66 - 1

LOS 16.g Explain
CFAI p. 144, Schweser p. 61

Aggregate Output, Prices, and Economic Growth

Aggregate Supply

In the **very short run**: Aggregate supply is elastic (input prices are fixed).

In the **short run**: Input prices are fixed so businesses expand real output when (output) prices increase.

In the **long run**: Aggregate supply is fixed at full-employment or potential real GDP.

67

Aggregate Supply

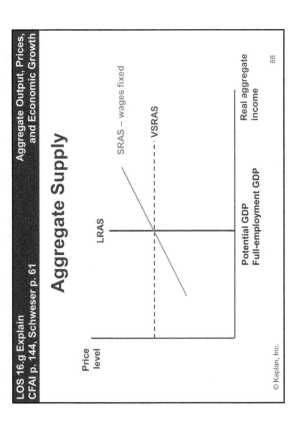

Shifts in Aggregate Demand

$$C + I + G + netX$$

- Increases in wealth increase C

- Increases in expectations for economic growth increase C, I

- Capacity utilization > ~85%⟶ increases I

- Increases in tax rates decrease disposable income and C

Aggregate Demand

The **aggregate demand curve** (AD) shows the relation between the price level and the real quantity of final goods and services (real GDP) demanded.

Components of aggregate demand:

- Consumption (C)
- Investment (I)
- Government spending (G)
- Net exports (X), exports minus imports

$$\boxed{\text{Aggregate demand} = C + I + G + _{net}X}$$

Shifts in Aggregate Demand

$$C + I + G + netX$$

- Increases in government spending, G

- Increases in the money supply reduce real rates and increase I, C

- Depreciation of currency increases netX, imports prices up, export prices down

- Growth of foreign GDP increases netX

LOS 16.h Explain
CFAI p. 146, Schweser p. 62

Shifts in LR Aggregate Supply

Factors that increase LRAS:

1. Increase in labor supply

2. Increased availability of natural resources

3. Increased stock of physical capital

4. Increased human capital (labor quality)

5. Advances in technology/labor productivity

© Kaplan, Inc.

73

LOS 16.i,j,k Describe/Distinguish/Explain
CFAI p. 158, Schweser p. 66

Aggregate Output, Prices, and Economic Growth

Decrease in Aggregate Demand

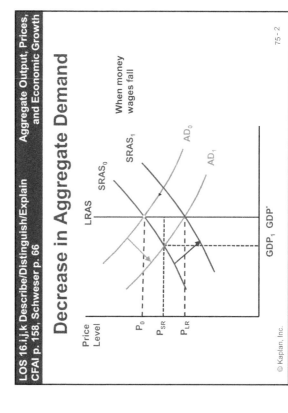

© Kaplan, Inc.

75 - 2

LOS 16.h Explain
CFAI p. 146, Schweser p. 62

Aggregate Output, Prices, and Economic Growth

Shifts in SR Aggregate Supply

Factors that increase SRAS:

1. Decreases in input prices

2. Improved expectations for economic growth

3. Decreases in business taxes

4. Increases in business subsidies

5. Currency appreciation that reduces the cost of imported inputs

© Kaplan, Inc.

72

LOS 16.i,j,k Describe/Distinguish/Explain
CFAI p. 158, Schweser p. 66

Aggregate Output, Prices, and Economic Growth

Increase in Aggregate Demand

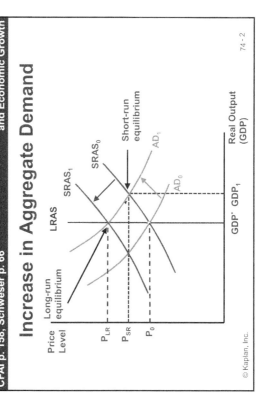

© Kaplan, Inc.

74 - 2

Stagflation

A supply shock decreases SRAS

Prices rise to P_1 and output declines to GDP_1

Government can address inflation or recession, not both

It can take a long, difficult time for wages and input prices to fall

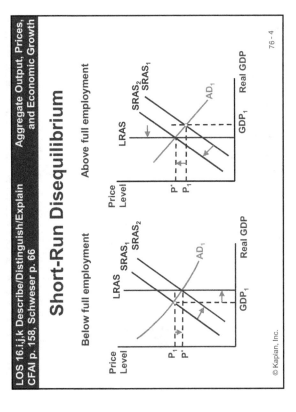

© Kaplan, Inc.

77

Sustainable Growth

Potential GDP =

Aggregate hours worked × labor productivity

Growth in potential GDP =
    growth in labor force +
    growth in labor productivity

Long-term equity returns are dependent on sustainable growth.

© Kaplan, Inc.

79

Short-Run Disequilibrium

Below full employment   Above full employment

© Kaplan, Inc.

76 - 4

Sources of Economic Growth

Same as factors that increase LRAS

1. Increase in labor supply

2. Increased availability of natural resources

3. Increased stock of physical capital

4. Increased human capital (labor quality)

5. Advances in technology/labor productivity

© Kaplan, Inc.

78

LOS 16.m Describe
CFAI p. 169, Schweser p. 71

Aggregate Output, Prices, and Economic Growth

Production Function Approach

$$Y = A \times f(L, K)$$

where:

Y = aggregate economic output

L = size of labor force

K = amount of capital available

A = total factor productivity, the increase in output not from increases in labor and capital, closely related to advances in technology

© Kaplan, Inc.

80

LOS 16.n Distinguish
CFAI p. 170, Schweser p. 72

Aggregate Output, Prices, and Economic Growth

Components of Economic Growth

Growth in potential GDP =

growth in total factor productivity +

W_C (growth in capital) +

W_L (growth in labor)

Where the weights are each factor's share of national income

© Kaplan, Inc.

81

LOS 16.n Distinguish
CFAI p. 170, Schweser p. 72

Aggregate Output, Prices, and Economic Growth

Per Capita Growth

Growth in per-capita potential GDP =

growth in technology +

W_C(growth in the _capital-to-labor ratio_)

In developed countries, *K/L* is high and growth in per capita GDP must come from technological advancement.

© Kaplan, Inc.

82

Aggregate Output, Prices, and Economic Growth

Growth of potential GDP has been 7% and labor's share of national income is 70%. The increase in the labor force has been 6% and the increase in the capital stock has been 5%. What is the increase in total factor productivity over the period?

© Kaplan, Inc.

83 - 2

Additional LOS

LOS 16.b: methods of calculating GDP

LOS 16.o: input growth and total factor productivity

85

Business Cycles

Cyclical behavior of GDP growth, inflation, and employment

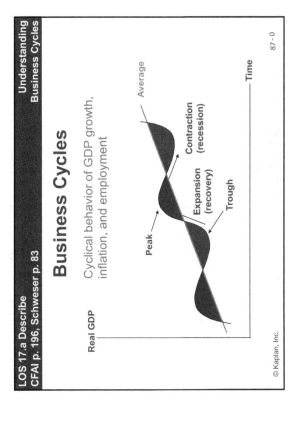

87 - 0

When the economy is operating at full-employment GDP, the short-run and long-run effects of an increase in the rate of growth of the money supply are to:

A. decrease real interest rates in the short run and increase real GDP in the long run.

B. increase real GDP in the short run but not in the long run.

C. increase the price level and real GDP in both the short and long run.

84 - 1

Microeconomics and Macroeconomics

17. Understanding Business Cycles

Slide 89

Business Cycle Theories

School of Thought	Cause of Business Cycles	Recommended Policy
Neoclassical	Technology changes	Allow wages, prices to adjust
Keynesian	AD shifts with changes in business expectations; contractions persist due to downward sticky wages	Use fiscal and/or monetary policy to restore full employment
New Keynesian	Same as Keynesian; but other input prices also downward sticky	Same as Keynesian

89

Slide 91

Types of Unemployment

Frictional unemployment results from time it takes employers and employees to find each other.

Structural unemployment results from long-term changes in the economy that require workers to gain new skills to fill new jobs.

Cyclical unemployment results from changes in economic growth; equals zero at full employment.

91

Slide 88 - 1

Based on typical labor utilization patterns across the business cycle, productivity (output per hours worked) is *most likely* to be highest:

A. at the peak of a boom.

B. into a maturing expansion

C. at the bottom of a recession.

88 - 1

Slide 90

Business Cycle Theories

School of Thought	Cause of Business Cycles	Recommended Policy
Monetarist	Inappropriate changes in money supply growth rate	Steady, predictable growth rate of money supply
Austrian	Government intervention in economy	Don't force interest rates to artificially low levels
New Classical (Real Business Cycle theory)	Rational responses to external shocks, technology changes	Don't intervene to counteract business cycles

90

Inflation, Disinflation, and Deflation

Inflation: Persistent increase in price level over time

Inflation rate: Percentage increase in price level over a period (usually one year)

Disinflation: Decrease in positive inflation rate over time

Deflation: Persistent decrease in price level over time; negative inflation rate

Hyperinflation: Out-of-control high inflation

© Kaplan, Inc.   93

Headline and Core Inflation

Price indexes that include all goods and services measure **headline inflation**.

Core inflation refers to prices of all goods excluding food and energy.

Food and energy prices are subject to large short-term fluctuations that can magnify or mask the true inflation rate.

© Kaplan, Inc.   95

Employment Measures

To be unemployed, one must be available for work **and** actively looking for work.

Labor force consists of those who are employed and those who are unemployed.

$$\text{Unemployment rate} = \frac{\text{Number of unemployed}}{\text{Labor force}}$$

$$\text{Participation ratio} = \frac{\text{Labor force}}{\text{Working-age population } (>16)}$$

Discouraged workers are not employed or seeking employment; **not counted in labor force.**

© Kaplan, Inc.   92

Calculating the CPI

1. Find the cost of the CPI basket in the base period
2. Find the cost of the CPI basket in the current period
3. Calculate the price index:

$$\text{CPI} = \frac{\text{cost of basket at current prices}}{\text{cost of basket at base year prices}} \times 100$$

Example: $\text{CPI} = \dfrac{\$2,900}{\$2,500} \times 100 = 116$ Prices up 16% over the period

© Kaplan, Inc.   94

LOS 17.g Compare
CFAI p. 225, Schweser p. 92

Limitations of Inflation Measures

The CPI is widely believed to **overstate** the true rate of inflation.

The most significant biases in the CPI data include:

- Consumer **substitution** of lower-priced products for higher-priced products

- **New goods** replace older, lower-priced products

- Price increases due to **quality improvements**

© Kaplan, Inc.

96

LOS 17.g Compare
CFAI p. 225, Schweser p. 92

Adjustments for CPI Bias

CPI is calculated using basket weights from base period (Laspeyres index).

A Paasche index uses basket weights from current period and compares cost to base period.

Chained price index reduces bias from substitution, for example:

Fisher index = geometric mean of Laspeyres and Paasche indexes

© Kaplan, Inc.

97

LOS 17.h Distinguish
CFAI p. 229, Schweser p. 94

Cost-Push Inflation (SRAS down)

Could result from an increase in real resource price

Stagflation without government intervention

© Kaplan, Inc.

98 - 2

LOS 17.h Distinguish
CFAI p. 229, Schweser p. 94

Demand-Pull Inflation (AD up)

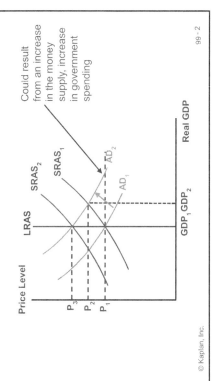

Could result from an increase in the money supply, increase in government spending

© Kaplan, Inc.

99 - 2

Additional Problems

Demand and Supply Analysis: Introduction

Additional LOS

LOS 17.i: uses and limitations of economic indicators

100

CFA Curriculum Vol. 2, R.15, Q.18, p. 108

2) In an industry comprised of three companies, which are small-scale manufacturers of an easily replicable product unprotected by brand recognition or patents, the *most* representative model of company behavior is:

   A. oligopoly.

   B. perfect competition.

   C. monopolistic competition.

-1

Additional Problems

1) A Giffen good is *best* described as a(n):

   A. inferior good for which a decrease in price will decrease quantity demanded.

   B. normal good for which an increase in price will increase quantity demanded.

   C. inferior good for which a decrease in price will increase quantity demanded.

-1

Additional Problems

4) The fundamental relationship between saving (S), investment (I), the fiscal balance (G – T), and the trade balance (X – M) is *best* represented by:

A. $S = I + (G - T) + (X - M)$.

B. $(X - M) = I - S - (G - T)$.

C. $(G - T) = (S - I) + (X - M)$.

-1

CFA Curriculum Vol. 2, R.15, Q.17, p. 108

3) One disadvantage of the Herfindahl-Hirschmann Index is that the index:

A. is difficult to compute.

B. fails to reflect low barriers to entry.

C. fails to reflect the effect of mergers in the industry.

-1

CFA Curriculum Vol. 2, R.17, Q.6, p. 245

5) The inventory/sales ratio is *most likely* to be rising:

A. as contraction unfolds.

B. partially into a recovery.

C. near the top of an economic cycle.

-1

STUDY SESSION 4 ANSWERS

Reading	Slide Number	Answer
14	7	B
14	12	A
14	18	C
15	26	C
15	45	C
16	56	A
16	57	C
16	65	C
16	66	B
16	83	1.3%
16	84	B
17	88	C

Additional Problems

1. A

2. B

3. B

4. A

5. C

Study Session 5

Economics: Monetary and Fiscal Policy, International Trade, and Currency Exchange Rates

Monetary and Fiscal Policy, International Trade, and Currency Exchange Rates

18. Monetary and Fiscal Policy

Study Session 5

Monetary and Fiscal Policy, International Trade, and Currency Exchange Rates

18. Monetary and Fiscal Policy
19. International Trade and Capital Flows
20. Currency Exchange Rates

Fiscal Policy

Government decisions on taxing and spending

Expansionary: Increase spending and/or decrease taxes; increase the budget deficit, increase aggregate demand

Contractionary: Decrease spending and/or increase taxes; decrease the budget deficit, reduce aggregate demand

3

Monetary Policy

Management of the supply of money and credit

Expansionary: Increasing the money supply decreases interest rates and increases aggregate demand

Contractionary: Decreasing the money supply increases interest rates and slows economic growth and inflation

2

LOS 18.e Describe   Monetary and Fiscal Policy
CFAI p. 266, Schweser p. 108

Fisher Effect

**Riskless nominal interest rate =
real riskless rate + expected inflation**

There is also uncertainty about future inflation rates
and other economic variables, and a risk premium
that increases with uncertainty

**Riskless nominal interest rate =
real riskless rate + expected inflation
+ risk premium for uncertainty**

© Kaplan, Inc.   5

LOS 18.d Describe   Monetary and Fiscal Policy
CFAI p. 263, Schweser p. 107

Equilibrium in the Money Market

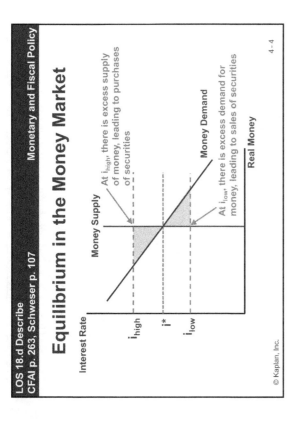

At i_{high}, there is excess supply
of money, leading to purchases
of securities

Money Supply

Money Demand

At i_{low}, there is excess demand for
money, leading to sales of securities

Interest Rate

i_{high}

i^*

i_{low}

Real Money

© Kaplan, Inc.   4 - 4

LOS 18.h Describe   Monetary and Fiscal Policy
CFAI p. 275, Schweser p. 111

Monetary Policy Tools

<u>Policy rate</u>: Interest rate central banks charge banks
for borrowed reserves

- By raising the policy rate, Fed discourages banks
  from borrowing reserves; thus, they reduce their
  lending
  - Decreasing the discount rate tends to increase the
    amount of lending and the money supply
  - The U.S. Fed sets a target for the fed funds rate,
    the rate at which banks lend short-term to each
    other

© Kaplan, Inc.   7

LOS 18.f Describe   Monetary and Fiscal Policy
CFAI p. 269, Schweser p. 109

Objectives of Central Banks

All central banks have price stability (low inflation
rates) as an objective. Many (except U.S. and
Japan) have explicit target rates, usually (2% to 3%).

<u>Some central banks also attempt to:</u>

- Maintain full employment
- Promote economic growth
- Keep exchange rates stable
- Keep long-term interest rates moderate

© Kaplan, Inc.   6

Monetary Policy Tools

<u>Open market operations</u>: *Most often used*

- Central bank buys government securities for cash, reserves increase, money supply increases
- Selling securities decreases the money supply

<u>Required reserve ratio</u>: *Seldom changed*

- Reducing required reserve percentage increases excess reserves and increases the money supply
- Increasing required reserve ratio decreases the money supply

© Kaplan, Inc.

8

Monetary Policy Transmission

<u>Expansionary monetary policy affects four things</u>:

1. Market interest rates fall, less incentive to save
2. Asset prices increase, wealth effect, consumption spending increases
3. Expectations for economic growth increase, may expect further decreases in interest rates
4. Domestic currency depreciates, import prices increase, export prices decrease

   Overall, aggregate demand increases, increasing real GDP, employment, and inflation

© Kaplan, Inc.

9

Central Bank Characteristics

To be **effective**, central banks should be:

1. **Independent**—free from political interference

   Not absolute; viewed as degree of independence

2. **Credible**: Bank follows through on stated intentions and policies

3. **Transparent**: Bank discloses inflation reports, indicators they use, and how they use them

© Kaplan, Inc.

10

Monetary Policy Effects on Economy

<u>When a central bank buys securities</u>:

- Bank reserves increase
- Interbank lending rates decrease
- Short-term and long-term lending rates decrease
- Businesses increase investment
- Consumers increase house, auto, and durable goods purchases
- Domestic currency depreciates, exports increase

  Overall, aggregate demand increases, increasing real GDP, employment, and inflation

© Kaplan, Inc.

11

LOS 18.l Contrast   Monetary and Fiscal Policy
CFAI p. 279, Schweser p. 115

Central Bank Targets

- **Interest rate targeting**: Increase (decrease) money supply growth when interest rates are above (below) targets

- **Inflation targeting**: Target band for inflation rate (typically 1% to 3%), inflation band > 0 to prevent deflation

- **Exchange rate targeting**: Target band for currency exchange rate with developed country

  Results in same inflation rate in domestic economy as in targeted developed country

12

LOS 18.m Describe   Monetary and Fiscal Policy
CFAI p. 288, Schweser p. 115

The Neutral Interest Rate

Neutral interest rate =
trend growth rate of real GDP
+ target inflation rate

Policy rate > neutral rate: <u>Contractionary</u>

Policy rate < neutral rate: <u>Expansionary</u>

13

CFA Curriculum Vol. 2,   Monetary and Fiscal Policy
R.18, Q.21, p. 321

Which of the following is a limitation on the ability of central banks to stimulate growth in periods of deflation?

A. Ricardian equivalence.

B. The interaction of monetary and fiscal policy.

C. The fact that interest rates have a minimum value (0%).

14 - 1

CFA Curriculum Vol. 2,   Monetary and Fiscal Policy
R.18, Q.22, p. 321

The *least likely* limitation to the effectiveness of monetary policy is that central banks cannot:

A. accurately determine the neutral rate of interest.

B. regulate the willingness of financial institutions to lend.

C. control amounts that economic agents deposit into banks.

15 - 1

Fiscal Policy

Keynesian economists believe that **discretionary fiscal policy** can stabilize the economy, increasing aggregate demand to combat recessions and decreasing aggregate demand to combat inflation

Monetarists believe that such effects are temporary and that appropriate monetary policy will dampen economic cycles

Automatic stabilizers (taxes and transfer payments) tend to increase deficits during recessions and decrease deficits during expansions

© Kaplan, Inc.   17

Fiscal Policy Tools: Revenue

Direct taxes—levied on income or wealth

Take time to implement

Indirect taxes—levied on goods and services

Quick to implement to raise revenue or promote social goals, or both (e.g., tobacco tax)

© Kaplan, Inc.   19

Fiscal Policy

Expansionary Fiscal Policy

Increase government spending, decrease taxes, or both—increasing aggregate demand and the budget deficit

Contractionary Fiscal Policy

Decrease government spending, increase taxes, or both—decreasing aggregate demand and the budget deficit

© Kaplan, Inc.   16

Fiscal Policy Tools: Spending

1. **Transfer payments**: Cash payments by government to redistribute wealth

2. **Current spending**: Purchases of goods and services

3. **Capital spending**: To increase future productivity; on infrastructure, or to support research on and development of new technologies

© Kaplan, Inc.   18

Fiscal Multiplier

Initial government spending has a multiplied effect as it creates more spending

Government purchases multiplier = $\dfrac{1}{1-MPC(1-t)}$

↑savings and ↑tax rate reduce the multiplier

For MPC = 0.8 and t = 0.3, a $100 billion spending increase, over time, can increase consumption by
1 / [1 − 0.8(1 − 0.3)] × $100 = $227 billion

20

Tax Multiplier

- With MPC = 0.8, a tax increase of $100 billion will reduce consumption by = 0.8 × 100 = $80 billion
- The fiscal multiplier effect will, over time, lead to a decrease in consumption spending of 2.27 × $80 billion = $182 billion

The **balanced budget multiplier** is positive

A $100 billion increase in spending + a $100 billion increase in taxes can, over time, increase consumption spending by $227 − $182 = $45 billion

21

Ricardian Equivalence

If a tax decrease causes taxpayers to increase savings in anticipation of higher future taxes, the resulting decrease in spending will reduce the expansionary impact of a tax cut

If the increase in saving (decrease in consumption) just offsets the tax decrease, it is termed **Ricardian equivalence**, and an increase in spending funded by issuing debt will have no impact on aggregate demand

22

Fiscal Policy Lags

Recognition lag: To identify the need for fiscal policy change

Action lag: To enact legislation

Impact lag: For the policy change to have the intended effect

Lags can cause fiscal policy changes to be destabilizing rather than stabilizing

23

Fiscal Policy Limitations

- If economy is at full employment, fiscal stimulus will result in higher inflation

- If economy is below full employment due to supply shortages, fiscal stimulus will lead to inflation rather than GDP growth

- If the economy has high unemployment and high inflation (stagflation), fiscal policy cannot address both

© Kaplan, Inc.   24

Analysis of Fiscal Policy

- Whether fiscal policy is expansionary or contractionary depends on the business cycle stage

- An adjusted, or full-employment, deficit amount can be used to adjust for the business cycle stage

In general:

Spending increases, tax decreases—**expansionary**
Spending decreases, tax increases—**contractionary**

© Kaplan, Inc.   25

Policy Interaction

- Monetary ↑ and Fiscal ↑: Strong expansionary effect, public and private sectors grow
- Monetary ↓ and Fiscal ↓: Decreased GDP growth, higher interest rates, public and private sectors decline
- Monetary ↑ and Fiscal ↓: Interest rates fall, consumption, output, and private sector expand
- Monetary ↓ and Fiscal ↑: Interest rates rise, aggregate demand likely higher, public sector portion of spending grows

© Kaplan, Inc.   26

The balanced budget multiplier is positive because:

A. the tax multiplier effect is stronger than the government purchases multiplier effect.

B. the government purchases multiplier effect is stronger than the tax multiplier effect.

C. The negative effect of the government purchases multiplier is less than the positive effect of the tax multiplier.

© Kaplan, Inc.   27 - 2

CFA Curriculum Vol. 2,
R.18, Q.31, p. 322 **Monetary and Fiscal Policy**

The *most likely* argument against high national debt levels is that:

A. the debt is owed internally to fellow citizens.

B. they create disincentives for economic activity.

C. they may finance investment in physical and human capital.

28 – 1

Economics

Monetary and Fiscal Policy, International Trade, and Currency Exchange Rates

19. International Trade and Capital Flows

KAPLAN UNIVERSITY SCHOOL OF PROFESSIONAL AND CONTINUING EDUCATION | **SCHWESER**

Additional LOS

Monetary and Fiscal Policy

LOS 18.b: functions and definitions of money

LOS 18.c: money creation process

LOS 18.g: expected and unexpected inflation

© Kaplan, Inc.

29

LOS 19.a Compare
CFAI p. 328, Schweser p. 135   **International Trade and Capital Flows**

Gross National Product (GNP) and Gross Domestic Product (GDP)

GDP is better for measuring domestic activity.

GDP: Value of goods and services produced <u>in</u> a country

GNP: Value of goods and services produced <u>by</u> a country's citizens

Differences:

- Income of citizens working abroad, non-citizens working in country

- Income to capital owned by foreigners, foreign capital owned by citizens

© Kaplan, Inc.

31 – 1

Benefits/Costs of International Trade

Benefits:

- Lower cost to consumers of imports
- Higher employment, wages, and profits in export industries

Costs:

Displacement of workers and lost profits in industries competing with imported goods

Economists: Benefits outweigh costs

© Kaplan, Inc.

32

Absolute vs. Comparative Advantage

Absolute advantage refers to lower cost in terms of resources used.

Comparative advantage refers to the lowest *opportunity* cost to produce a product.

Law of comparative advantage:

- Trade makes **all countries better off.**
- Each country specializes in goods they produce most efficiently and trades for other goods.

Outcome: Increased worldwide output and wealth with no country being worse off

© Kaplan, Inc.

33

Absolute vs. Comparative Advantage

Labor costs per unit produced	Cloth	Wine
England	100	110
Portugal	90	80

Portugal has absolute advantage in both wine and cloth.

England has comparative advantage in cloth; opportunity cost of cloth is 10/11 wine in England vs. 9/8 wine in Portugal.

Portugal has comparative advantage in wine; opportunity cost of wine is 8/9 cloth in Portugal vs. 11/10 in England.

© Kaplan, Inc.

34

Absolute vs. Comparative Advantage

Opportunity cost per unit	Cloth	Wine
England	10/11-Wine	11/10-Cloth
Portugal	9/8-Wine	8/9-Cloth

If **Portugal specializes in wine** production and **England specializes in cloth** production, both can be better off.

Trade can also produce benefits from economies of scale and efficiencies resulting from cross-border competition.

© Kaplan, Inc.

35

Models of Trade

Ricardian model

- Labor is the only factor of production.
- Comparative advantage depends on relative labor productivity for different goods.

Heckscher-Ohlin model

- Two factors of production: capital and labor
- Comparative advantage depends on relative amount of each factor possessed by a country.

© Kaplan, Inc.

36

Heckscher-Ohlin Model

Under Heckscher-Ohlin model, there is a redistribution of wealth between the two factors of production due to international trade.

The price of the more abundant resource will increase as more of it is used to produce exports.

Results in a **wealth transfer** within a country from owners of the scarce resource (labor or capital) to owners of the abundant resource.

© Kaplan, Inc.

37

Trade Restrictions

Tariff is a tax imposed on imported goods.

Quota is a limitation on the quantity of goods imported.

Export subsidies are payments by government to domestic exporters.

Minimum domestic content specifies required proportion of product content to be sourced domestically.

Voluntary export restraints (VERs) are agreements by exporting countries to limit the quantity of goods they will export to an importing country.

© Kaplan, Inc.

38

Effects of Tariffs and Quotas

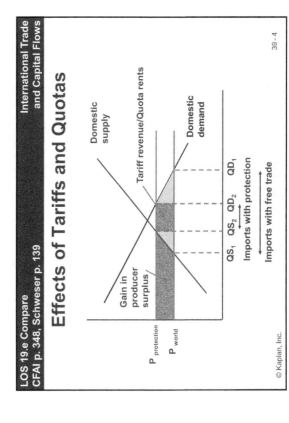

© Kaplan, Inc.

39 - 4

Trade Restrictions

Trade Restriction	Domestic Consumer	Domestic Producer	Domestic Government	Foreign Exporter
Tariff	Loses	Gains	Gains	Loses
Quota	Loses	Gains	Gains[1]	Gains[1]
VER	Loses	Gains	None	Gains
Export Subsidy	Loses	Gains	Loses	NA

1. In case of quotas, the distribution of gains between the domestic government and the foreign exporter depends on the amount of **quota rent** collected by the domestic government.

© Kaplan, Inc.

41

Objectives of Capital Restrictions

Reduce volatility of domestic asset prices due to large inflows and outflows of capital

Maintain exchange-rate target while using monetary and fiscal policy for domestic goals

Keep domestic interest rates low by restricting outflows of capital to higher-yielding foreign investments

Protect strategic industries (e.g., defense) from foreign ownership

© Kaplan, Inc.

43

Reasons for Trade Restrictions

Two primary goals:
1. Protecting domestic jobs
2. Protecting domestic producers

- Other reasons include countering foreign trade restrictions and export subsidies, anti-dumping, and revenues from tariff for domestic government.

- A large country could actually decrease the world price by imposing a quota or tariff.

© Kaplan, Inc.

40

Capital Restrictions

Restrictions on flow of financial capital:
- Outright prohibition
- Punitive taxation
- Restrictions on repatriation

Restrictions decrease economic welfare.

Short-term benefit for developing countries: reducing volatile capital inflows and outflows

Long-term costs: isolation from global capital markets

© Kaplan, Inc.

42

Balance of Payments (BOP) Accounts

Current Account

Merchandise/services purchases, foreign dividends and interest, and unilateral transfers

Capital Account

Sales/purchases of physical assets, natural resources, intangible assets, debt forgiveness, death duties, and taxes

Financial Account

Domestic-owned financial assets abroad (official reserve, government, private) and foreign-owned domestic financial assets

© Kaplan, Inc.

44

BOP Influences

From $S - I = (G - T) + (X - M)$

$X - M = (S - I) + (T - G)$ or

= private savings − investment + government savings

An increase (decrease) in **private or government savings** would improve (worsen) the balance of trade.

A trade deficit due to a decrease in private or government savings is less desirable than a trade deficit due to high domestic investment.

© Kaplan, Inc.

45

Additional LOS

LOS 19.f: trading blocs, common markets, economic unions

LOS 19.j: international trade organizations

© Kaplan, Inc.

46

Monetary and Fiscal Policy, International Trade, and Currency Exchange Rates

20. Currency Exchange Rates

KAPLAN UNIVERSITY   SCHOOL OF PROFESSIONAL AND CONTINUING EDUCATION   **SCHWESER**

Real Exchange Rate

Base period: 1/1/X1 exchange rate = 1.20 $/€
            1/1/X3 exchange rate = 1.30 $/€

Base period: 1/1/X1 CPI$_{USD}$ = 100; CPI$_{euro}$ = 100
            On 1/1/X3, CPI$_{USD}$ = 114; CPI$_{euro}$ = 109

Calculate the real exchange rate on 1/1/X3.

real exchange rate (p/b) = nominal exchange rate (p/b) × $\left(\dfrac{CPI_{base}}{CPI_{price}} \right)$

= 1.30 × 109 / 114 = 1.243 $/€

> The real cost of euro zone goods to a U.S. citizen has gone
> up by 1.243 / 1.20 − 1 = 3.6%; which is less than the nominal
> rate has gone up (8.3%) because U.S. inflation was higher.

© Kaplan, Inc.   49 – 3

Market Participants

Hedgers

> Have an existing FX risk that they want to
> reduce/eliminate with forward FX contracts

Speculators

> Are not hedging an existing FX risk

> Take on FX risk with forward contracts with
> the expectation of earning a profit

© Kaplan, Inc.   51

Foreign Exchange Quotations

0.5440 GBP/USD means £0.5440 **per USD**

| Price currency | | Base currency |

Nominal exchange rate is the quoted rate at
any point in time.

Real exchange rate is the nominal exchange
rate adjusted for inflation in each country
compared to a base period.

real exchange rate (p/b) = nominal exchange rate (p/b) × $\left(\dfrac{CPI_{base}}{CPI_{price}} \right)$

© Kaplan, Inc.   48

Spot Market vs. Forward Market

Spot exchange rates: Exchange rates for
immediate delivery

Forward contract: An agreement to buy or sell
a specific amount of a foreign currency at a
future date at the quoted <u>forward exchange
rate</u> (e.g., 30, 60, or 90 days in the future)

© Kaplan, Inc.   50

Market Participants

Sell side

Market makers: Large multinational banks

Buy side

- Corporations
- Investment accounts: Real money and leveraged
- Governments, sovereign wealth funds, pension plans, central banks
- Retail market: Households (e.g., tourism)

© Kaplan, Inc.

52

Currency Appreciation or Depreciation

Consider a **USD/GBP** exchange rate that has gone **down** from 1.61 to 1.59.

The USD price of a British pound has gone **down** $1.59 / 1.61 - 1 = -1.24\%$, and we say the pound has depreciated relative to the USD by 1.24%.

The GBP/USD exchange rate has gone **up** from $1 / 1.61 = 0.6211$ to $1 / 1.59 = 0.6289$.

The GBP price of a USD has gone **up** by $0.6289 / 0.6211 - 1 = 1.26\%$, and we say the USD has appreciated relative to the GBP by 1.26%.

© Kaplan, Inc.

53

Cross Rates Example

Given the following FX rates:

1.5600 USD/GBP and **1.4860 CHF/USD**

Calculate the **CHF/GBP** cross rate.

$$\frac{USD}{GBP} \times \frac{CHF}{USD} = \frac{CHF}{GBP}$$

Set up the quotes so the common currency cancels

$$1.5600 \, \frac{USD}{GBP} \times 1.4860 \, \frac{CHF}{USD} = 2.3182 \, \frac{CHF}{GBP}$$

© Kaplan, Inc.

54 - 3

Forward Quotes—Point Basis

Forward quote is points above (below) spot

Point is last digit of the spot rate quote

Last digit is 0.0001

Spot 1.4320 \$/€, Forward quote + **22.1** points

Forward = $1.4320 + $ **22.1(0.0001)** $= 1.43421$ \$/€

© Kaplan, Inc.

55

Forward Quotes—Percentage Basis

Spot 1.6135 $/£

90-day forward quote is –0.29%

Forward = 1.6135 (1 – 0.0029) = $1.6088 $/£

We say the U.S. dollar is **trading at a forward premium** relative to the British pound.

If the forward quote is –47 points, **percentage forward quote** is –0.0047 / 1.6135 = –0.0029 = –0.29%.

© Kaplan, Inc.

56

Forward Discount or Premium

For FX quote of price currency / base currency

If the forward quote is greater than spot price:

Base currency is trading at **forward premium**

Price currency is trading at a **forward discount**

If the forward quote is less than spot price:

Base currency is trading at **forward discount**

Price currency is trading at a **forward premium**

© Kaplan, Inc.

57

If the base currency in a forward exchange rate quote is trading at a forward discount, which of the following statements is *most* accurate?

A. The forward points will be positive.

B. The forward percentage will be negative.

C. The base currency is expected to appreciate versus the price currency.

58 - 1

No-Arbitrage Forward Exchange Rate

$$\frac{\text{Forward}(P/B)}{\text{Spot}(P/B)} = \frac{1 + \text{Interest Rate}_{price}}{1 + \text{Interest Rate}_{base}}$$

Follow the Numerator-Denominator rule:
Given a quote as price/base, use interest rate of price currency in numerator and interest rate of base currency in the denominator

© Kaplan, Inc.

59

No-Arbitrage Forward Rate

Spot rate = 1.50 $/£; Riskless $ interest rate is 2%; Riskless £ interest rate is 2.5%. **Calculate** the arbitrage-free 1-year forward rate.

$$\text{Forward}(\$/£) = \left[\frac{1+\text{Interest Rate}_\$}{1+\text{Interest Rate}_£}\right] \times \text{Spot}(\$/£)$$

$$= \left[\frac{1+0.02}{1+0.025}\right] \times 1.50 = 1.4927 \ \$/£$$

U.K. interest rate is higher, so forward $ / £ is less than spot $ / £.

© Kaplan, Inc.

60

The 90-day euro Libor is 3% and the 90-day AUD Libor is 4% (both annualized rates).

The spot EUR/AUD rate is 0.7276. The 90-day forward AUD/EUR no-arbitrage rate is *closest* to:

A. 1.3877.

B. 1.3778.

C. 1.3710.

© Kaplan, Inc.

61 - 3

Exchange Rates, Trade, and Capital

(X – M) = (private savings – investment) + (tax revenue – government spending)

(X – M) > 0, trade surplus when private savings + government surplus exceeds domestic investment

(X – M) < 0, trade deficit when private savings – domestic investment is less than budget deficit

© Kaplan, Inc.

62

Exchange Rates and Trade Deficit

Elasticities Approach

$$W_M = \frac{\text{Imports}}{\text{Imports} + \text{Exports}} \qquad W_X = \frac{\text{Exports}}{\text{Imports} + \text{Exports}}$$

ε_X and ε_M are demand elasticities

Classic Marshall-Lerner condition

$$\varepsilon_X + \varepsilon_M > 1$$

If the sum of export and import elasticities is large enough, then currency depreciation will reduce trade deficit.

© Kaplan, Inc.

63

Exchange Rates and Trade Deficit

J-Curve Effect

In the short run, due to existing contracts, export and import demand are relatively inelastic.

➤ Currency depreciation initially leads to a larger trade deficit.

In the long run, elasticities increase.

➤ Currency depreciation leads to a reduction in the trade deficit.

© Kaplan, Inc.

64

Exchange Rates and Trade Deficit

The elasticities approach only considers goods flows.

The absorption approach includes the effect of currency depreciation on capital flows, as well as trade flows.

© Kaplan, Inc.

65

Additional LOS

LOS 20.i: exchange rate regimes

© Kaplan, Inc.

66

Additional Problems

KAPLAN
UNIVERSITY   SCHOOL OF PROFESSIONAL
AND CONTINUING EDUCATION   SCHWESER

Additional Problems

1) Limitations on the ability of expansionary fiscal policy to increase real GDP *least likely* include:

   A. resource constraints.

   B. reduced consumption due to increased taxes.

   C. reduced private investment due to government borrowing.

-1

CFA Curriculum Vol. 2,
R.18, Q.32, p. 322

3) Which statement regarding fiscal deficits is *most* accurate?

   A. Higher government spending may lead to higher interest rates and lower private sector investing.

   B. Central bank actions that grow the money supply to address deflationary conditions decrease fiscal deficits.

   C. According to the Ricardian equivalence, deficits have a multiplicative effect on consumer spending.

-1

CFA Curriculum Vol. 2,
R.16, Q.33, p. 190

2) An economic forecasting firm has estimated the following equation from historical data based on the neoclassical growth model:

   Potential output growth = 1.5
   + 0.72 × Growth of labor
   + 0.28 × Growth of capital

   The intercept (1.5) in this equation is *best* interpreted as:

   A. the long-run sustainable growth rate.

   B. the growth rate of total factor productivity.

   C. above trend historical growth that is unlikely to be sustained.

-1

CFA Curriculum Vol. 2,
R.19, Q.16, p. 386

4) The sale of mineral rights would be captured in which of the following balance of payments components?

   A. Capital account.

   B. Current account.

   C. Financial account.

-1

CFA Curriculum Vol. 2,
R.19, Q.17, p. 386

5) Patent fees and legal services are recorded in which of the following balance of payments components?

A. Capital account.

B. Current account.

C. Financial account.

- 1

CFA Curriculum Vol. 2,
R.19, Q.19, p. 386

6) Which of the following *most likely* contributes to a current account deficit?

A. High taxes.

B. Low private savings.

C. Low private investment.

- 1

CFA Curriculum Vol. 2,
R.20, Q.7, p. 449

7) Over the past month, the Swiss Franc (CHF) has depreciated 12 percent against pound sterling (GBP). How much has the pound sterling appreciated against the Swiss franc?

A. 12%.

B. Less than 12%.

C. More than 12%.

- 2

CFA Curriculum Vol. 2,
R.20, Q.20, p. 451

8) A large industrialized country has recently devalued its currency in an attempt to correct a persistent trade deficit. Which of the following domestic industries is *most likely* to benefit from the devaluation?

A. Luxury cars.

B. Branded prescription drugs.

C. Restaurants and live entertainment venues.

- 2

Additional Problems

9) The EUR/USD exchange rate fell from 0.897 to 0.874. Relative to the USD, the euro has appreciated by:

A. 2.36%.

B. 2.56%.

C. 2.63%.

- 1

STUDY SESSION 5 ANSWERS

Reading	Slide Number	Answer
18	14	C
18	15	A
18	27	B
18	28	B
20	58	B
20	61	B

Additional Problems

1. B

2. B

3. A

4. A

5. B

6. B

7. C

8. A

9. C

Study Session 6

Financial Reporting and Analysis: An Introduction

Financial Reporting and Analysis: An Introduction

21. Financial Statement Analysis: An Introduction

KAPLAN UNIVERSITY | SCHOOL OF PROFESSIONAL AND CONTINUING EDUCATION | SCHWESER

Study Session 6
Financial Reporting and Analysis: An Introduction

21. Financial Statement Analysis: An Introduction
22. Financial Reporting Mechanics
23. Financial Reporting Standards

KAPLAN UNIVERSITY | SCHOOL OF PROFESSIONAL AND CONTINUING EDUCATION | SCHWESER

© Kaplan, Inc.

LOS 21.a Describe
CFAI p. 6, Schweser p. 1

Role of Financial Statement Analysis

Using the information in a company's financial statements, along with other relevant information, to make economic decisions (e.g., evaluate securities, acquisitions, creditworthiness)

To evaluate a company's past performance and current financial position in order to form opinions about a firm's ability to earn profits and generate cash flow in the future

© Kaplan, Inc.

3

LOS 21.a Describe
CFAI p. 6, Schweser p. 1

Role of Financial Reporting

"The objective of general purpose financial reporting is to provide financial information about the reporting entity that is useful to existing and potential investors, lenders, and other creditors in making decisions about providing resources to the entity. Those decisions involve buying, selling or holding equity and debt instruments, and providing or settling loans and other forms of credit."

IASB Conceptual Framework

© Kaplan, Inc.

2

Key Financial Statements

2. **Statement of comprehensive income** reports all changes in equity other than shareholder transactions for the period

3. **Balance sheet (statement of financial position)** at a point in time
   - Assets = liabilities + owners' equity
   - *Assets* are the resources controlled by the firm
   - *Liabilities* are amounts owed to lenders and other creditors
     - *Owners' equity* is the residual interest in a firm's assets that remains after deducting its liabilities

© Kaplan, Inc.   5

Footnotes and Supplementary Schedules

- Basis of presentation
- Accounting methods and assumptions
- Further information on amounts in primary statements
- Business acquisitions/disposals
- Contingencies
- Legal proceedings
- Stock options and benefit plans
- Significant customers
- Segment data
- Quarterly data
- Related-party transactions

© Kaplan, Inc.   7

Key Financial Statements

1. **Income statement** (statement of operations or profit and loss statement) summarizes events over a period.

   Revenues are inflows from delivering or producing goods, rendering services, or other activities that constitute the entity's ongoing major or central operations.

   Expenses are outflows from delivering or producing goods or services that constitute the entity's ongoing major or central operations.

   Other income includes **gains and losses** which may or may not arise in ordinary course of business.

© Kaplan, Inc.   4

Key Financial Statements

4. **Cash flow statement** reconciles beginning and ending cash balance; changes are divided into three categories:
   - *Operating cash flows (CFO)*
   - *Investing cash flows (CFI)*
   - *Financing cash flows (CFF)*

5. **Statement of changes in owners' equity** amounts and sources of changes in shareholders' equity over the period

© Kaplan, Inc.   6

Management Discussion and Analysis

- Nature of the business
- Results from operations, business overview
- Trends in sales and expenses
- Capital resources and liquidity
- Cash flow trends
- Discussion of critical accounting choices
- Effects of inflation, price changes, and uncertainties on future results

© Kaplan, Inc.

8

The Audit Report

- **Audit:** *Independent review* of company's financial statements
- **Reasonable assurance** that financial statements are free of material errors
- **Audit opinion:**
  - Unqualified: "Clean" opinion
  - Qualified: Exceptions to accounting principles
  - Adverse: Statements not presented fairly
  - Disclaimer of opinion: Unable to form an opinion
- Must provide opinion on company's **internal controls** under U.S. GAAP

© Kaplan, Inc.

9

Audit Report

1. Responsibility of management to prepare accounts; independence of auditors
2. Properly prepared in accordance with relevant GAAP; reasonable assurance that the statements are free from material misstatement
3. Accounting principles and estimates chosen are reasonable

© Kaplan, Inc.

10

Regarding the report of independent auditors under U.S. GAAP, the audit report:

A. is unqualified if the auditors disagree with the firm on the treatment of some items.

B. must provide an opinion on the firm's internal controls.

C. does not apply to the footnotes to the financial statements.

© Kaplan, Inc.

11 - 1

Financial Reporting and Analysis: An Introduction

22. Financial Reporting Mechanics

KAPLAN UNIVERSITY   SCHOOL OF PROFESSIONAL AND CONTINUING EDUCATION | SCHWESER

LOS 22.b Explain/Classify
CFAI p. 44, Schweser p. 11

Common Asset Accounts

- Cash and cash equivalents
- Accounts receivable, trade receivables
- Prepaid expenses
- Inventory
- Property, plant, and equipment (PP&E)
- Investment property
- Intangibles
- Financial assets (investment securities)
- Investments under the equity method
- Deferred tax assets

© Kaplan, Inc.

15

Additional LOS

LOS 21.e: information sources
LOS 21.f: financial statement analysis framework

© Kaplan, Inc.

12

LOS 22.a Describe
CFAI p. 42, Schweser p. 10

Classification of Business Activities

Operating Activities
- Part of the firm's regular business operations
- Creating and selling product or service
- Making a loan is an operating activity for a bank, but not for a manufacturer or other non-financial firm

Investing Activities
The purchase and sale of long-term assets (e.g., building, securities, factory, truck)

Financing Activities
Raising and repayment of capital (e.g., issuance or repurchase of stock, issuing or redeeming bonds, taking or repayment of a bank loan)

© Kaplan, Inc.

14

Common Liability Accounts

- Accounts payable, trade payables
- Provisions/accrued liabilities
- Financial liabilities
- Current and deferred tax
- Unearned revenue
- Debt payable
- Bonds

© Kaplan, Inc.

16

Common Equity Accounts

- Capital at par value
- Additional paid-in capital
- Retained earnings
- Other comprehensive income
- Noncontrolling (minority) interest

© Kaplan, Inc.

17

Common Income Statement Items

Revenue
- Sales
- Gains
- Investment income

Expense
- Cost of goods sold
- SG&A (selling, general, and admin)
- Depreciation/amortization
- Interest
- Tax expense
- Losses

© Kaplan, Inc.

18

Accounting Equations

Revenue – Expenses = Net income

Assets = Liabilities + Owners' equity

Assets – Liabilities = Owners' equity

Owners' equity = Contributed capital + Retained earnings

© Kaplan, Inc.

19

Financial Reporting Mechanics

LOS 22.c Explain
CFAI p. 46, Schweser p. 12

Accounting Equations

	$m
Beginning retained earnings	X
Net income (loss)	X
Dividends	(X)
Ending retained earnings	X

© Kaplan, Inc.

20

Financial Reporting Mechanics

LOS 22.d Describe
CFAI p. 51, Schweser p. 13

Accounting for Transactions

1. Pay a bill $E = A - L$

Asset "cash" goes down.

Liability "trade payables" goes down.

Equity is unchanged.

2. Issue a bond (borrow money) $E = A - L$

Asset "cash" goes up by proceeds.

Liability "bonds payable" goes up by proceeds.

Equity is unchanged.

© Kaplan, Inc.

21

Financial Reporting Mechanics

LOS 22.d Describe
CFAI p. 51, Schweser p. 13

Accounting for Transactions

3. Make a credit sale $E = A - L$

Asset "inventory" goes down.

Asset "accounts receivable" goes up by more.

Equity "retained earnings" increases by difference.

On the income statement

Revenues increase, expenses increase by less.

Net income and retained earnings increase.

Retained earnings is an equity account.

© Kaplan, Inc.

22

Financial Reporting Mechanics

LOS 22.d Describe
CFAI p. 51, Schweser p. 13

Accounting for Transactions

4. Buy materials on credit $E = A - L$

Asset "inventory" increases.

Liability "accounts payable" increases.

Equity is unchanged.

5. Issue stock $E = A - L$

Asset "cash" goes up.

Liabilities unchanged.

Equity "common stock" increases.

© Kaplan, Inc.

23

Accounting for Transactions

6. Incur an expense $E = A - L$

Liability increases.

Assets are unchanged.

Equity "retained earnings" decreases.

7. Pay a liability $E = A - L$

Asset "cash" goes down.

Liability goes down.

Equity is unchanged.

© Kaplan, Inc.

24

Statements and Security Analysis

Financial statements contain:

- Estimates   ⎤
- Judgements   ⎦ Accruals and valuations

Analyst must review:

- MDA   ⎤
- Footnotes ⎦ Critical accounting policies and estimates sections

Analyst must make appropriate adjustments for analysis.

© Kaplan, Inc.

25

Which of the following would be *most likely* to change equity?

A. Collecting receivables

B. Selling a 5-year-old machine

C. Declaring a dividend

© Kaplan, Inc.

26 - 2

Additional LOS

LOS 22.e: accruals and other adjustments

LOS 22.f: relationships among statements

LOS 22.g: flow of information in an accounting system

© Kaplan, Inc.

27

Financial Reporting and Analysis

Financial Reporting and Analysis: An Introduction

23. Financial Reporting Standards

KAPLAN UNIVERSITY SCHOOL OF PROFESSIONAL AND CONTINUING EDUCATION | SCHWESER

LOS 23.b Describe
CFAI p. 103, Schweser p. 26

Accounting Standards

Financial Accounting Standards Board (FASB) – U.S.

International Accounting Standards Board (IASB) – many other countries

© Kaplan, Inc.

29

LOS 23.b Describe
CFAI p. 103, Schweser p. 26

Financial Reporting Requirements and Regulation

Regulation of markets, financial reporting, and public issuance of securities

- U.S. Securities and Exchange Commission (SEC)
- Each EU member state has its own securities regulation
- European Securities and Market Authority (ESMA) coordinates supervision of EU members' regulators

© Kaplan, Inc.

30

LOS 23.b Describe
CFAI p. 103, Schweser p. 26

Financial Reporting Requirements and Regulation

International Organization of Securities Commissions (IOSCO)—members represent 90% of all capital markets worldwide

Core objectives:
- Protect investors
- Fair, efficient, and transparent markets
- Reduction of systemic risk

© Kaplan, Inc.

31

Global Convergence of Accounting Standards

Convergence refers to reducing differences in worldwide accounting standards.

1. Increase comparability

2. Decrease problems and expenses of raising capital in foreign markets

3. Decrease problems and expenses of preparing consolidated financial statements for foreign subsidiaries

Accounting standards in most major countries are converging over time with IFRS.

© Kaplan, Inc.   32

Barriers to Standards Convergence

- **Differences in view** between standard setting bodies
- **Pressure** from business and industry groups
- Many **different countries involved**, different institutions, cultures, business environments, systems of regulation

If the application and enforcement of accounting standards differ, convergence in standards is not enough to ensure comparability of statements.

© Kaplan, Inc.   33

IFRS Conceptual Framework

Two qualitative characteristics for "decision useful" financial reporting:

1. Relevance

   The information can influence users' economic decisions, affect users' evaluations of past events, or affect forecasts of future events.

   Information should have predictive value, confirm prior expectations, or both. **Materiality** is an aspect of relevance.

© Kaplan, Inc.   34

IFRS Conceptual Framework

2. Faithful representation

   Information that is faithfully represented is complete, neutral (absence of bias), and free from error.

   The following characteristics enhance these two primary qualitative characteristics:

   - Comparability
   - Verifiability
   - Timeliness
   - Understandability

© Kaplan, Inc.   35

LOS 23.d Describe
CFAI p. 115, Schweser p. 28   Financial Reporting Standards

Constraints

While it would be ideal to have all characteristics, in reality there are trade-offs:

Relevance versus verifiability

Benefits versus costs

Excludes non-quantifiable information

© Kaplan, Inc.   36

LOS 23.g Identify
CFAI p. 128, Schweser p. 32   Financial Reporting Standards

Characteristics of a Coherent Reporting Framework

Transparency

- Accounts reflect economic substance
- Full disclosure and fair presentation

Comprehensiveness

- Full spectrum of financial transactions
- Framework flexible enough to adapt to new transactions

Consistency

- Transactions measured and presented in a similar way (across companies and time)
- Sufficient flexibility to show economic substance

© Kaplan, Inc.   37

LOS 23.g Identify
CFAI p. 128, Schweser p. 32   Financial Reporting Standards

Barriers to a Single Coherent Framework

1. Valuation
   - Historic cost: Minimal judgement—reliable
   - Fair value: Considerable judgement—relevant

2. Standard setting
   - Principles-based—few specific rules, requires judgement
   - Rules-based—prescriptive but not flexible
   - Objectives-based—combines principles and rules

© Kaplan, Inc.   38

LOS 23.g Identify
CFAI p. 128, Schweser p. 32   Financial Reporting Standards

Barriers to a Single Framework

3. Measurement
   - **Asset/liability approach** results in better balance sheet information
   - **Revenue/expense approach**, focus on income statement

   Standards regarding one statement will have an effect on the other—approaches may conflict.

   Standard setters have favored the asset/liability approach most recently.

© Kaplan, Inc.   39

LOS 23.i Analyze
CFAI p. 133, Schweser p. 33   Financial Reporting Standards

Company Disclosures

- Critical and significant accounting policies
- Accounting estimates
- Changes in accounting policy
- Footnote disclosure and discussion in MD&A

Analyst focus:

- What policies have been discussed?
- Do the policies cover all significant transactions?
- Which balances require significant estimation?
- Have there been changes?

© Kaplan, Inc.

40

Financial Reporting Standards

Additional LOS

LOS 23.a: objective of financial statements, importance of financial reporting standards

LOS 23.e: general requirements under IFRS

LOS 23.f: IFRS and U.S. GAAP

LOS 23.h: monitoring developments in financial reporting standards

© Kaplan, Inc.

41

Financial Reporting and Analysis

Additional Problems

CFA Curriculum Vol. 3,
R.23, Q.6, p. 140

1) According to the *Conceptual Framework for Financial Reporting (2010)*, which of the following is *not* an enhancing qualitative characteristic of information in financial statements?

A. Accuracy.

B. Timeliness.

C. Comparability.

-1

CFA Curriculum Vol. 3,
R.23, Q.17, p. 141

3) Which of the following is *not* a recognized approach to standard-setting?

A. A rules-based approach.

B. An asset/liability approach.

C. A principles-based approach.

- 1

Additional Problems   **Financial Reporting Standards**

5) An investor would *most likely* prefer that a firm receive an audit opinion of:

A. adverse.

B. qualified.

C. unqualified.

- 1

CFA Curriculum Vol. 3,
R.23, Q.16, p. 141

2) Which of the following is *not* a characteristic of a coherent financial reporting framework?

A. Timeliness.

B. Consistency.

C. Transparency.

- 1

Reference Level I CFA Curriculum,
Reading 22, Problem 9

4) A company paid 20,000 on December 31, 20X1 to cover January and February rent of 8,000/mo. and a security deposit of 4,000. The *most likely* impact of this payment on reported 20X1 year-end assets is:

A. no change.

B. a decrease of 16,000.

C. a decrease of 20,000.

- 2

CFA Curriculum Vol. 3,
R.21, Q.4, p. 38

6) Accounting policies, methods, and estimates used in preparing financial statements are *most likely* to be found in the:

A. auditor's report.

B. management commentary.

C. notes to the financial statements.

- 1

STUDY SESSION 6 ANSWERS

Reading	Slide Number	Answer
21	11	B
22	26	C

Additional Problems

1. A

2. A

3. B

4. A

5. C

6. C

Study Session 7

Financial Reporting and Analysis: Income Statements, Balance Sheets, and Cash Flow Statements

Income Statements, Balance Sheets, and Cash Flow Statements

24. Understanding Income Statements

KAPLAN UNIVERSITY | SCHOOL OF PROFESSIONAL AND CONTINUING EDUCATION | SCHWESER

© Kaplan, Inc.

Study Session 7
Income Statements, Balance Sheets, and Cash Flow Statements

24. Understanding Income Statements
25. Understanding Balance Sheets
26. Understanding Cash Flow Statements
27. Financial Analysis Techniques

KAPLAN UNIVERSITY | SCHOOL OF PROFESSIONAL AND CONTINUING EDUCATION | SCHWESER

© Kaplan, Inc.

LOS 24.a Describe
CFAI p. 149, Schweser p. 39   Understanding Income Statements

Income Statement

Revenues: Amounts reported from the sale of goods and services in the normal course of business.

Revenue less adjustments for estimated returns and allowances is known as **net revenue.**

Expenses: Amounts incurred to generate revenue and include cost of goods sold, operating expenses, interest, and taxes.

Gains and losses: Typically arise on the disposal of long-lived assets

© Kaplan, Inc.

3

LOS 24.a Describe
CFAI p. 149, Schweser p. 39   Understanding Income Statements

Income Statement

Statement of operations

Statement of earnings

Profit and loss statement

| Revenue – Expenses = Net Income |

Two types:
- Single step
- Multi-step

IFRS: May combine with comprehensive income items

© Kaplan, Inc.

2

Multi-step Income Statement

Revenue
- Cost of goods sold

Gross profit
- Selling, general, and administrative expenses

Operating profit
+ Other income and revenues
- Financing costs
+/- Unusual or infrequent items

Income before tax

> Operating or non-operating? Analyze items

Multi-step Income Statement

Income before tax
- Provision for income taxes   "The line"

Income from continuing operations   All net

+/- Income from discontinued operations   of tax
+/- Extraordinary items
   Net income   "The bottom line"

IASB Requirements for Revenue Recognition (General Principles)

1. Risk and reward of ownership transferred
2. No continuing control or management over the good sold
3. Reliable revenue measurement
4. Probable flow of economic benefits
5. Cost can be measured reliably

IASB Requirements for Revenue Recognition for Services

1. When the outcome can be measured reliably, revenue will be recognized by reference to the stage of completion.
2. Outcome can be measured reliably if:
   - Amount of revenue can be measured.
   - Probable flow of economic benefits.
   - Stage of completion can be measured.
   - Cost incurred and remaining cost to complete can be measured.

SEC Requirements for Revenue Recognition

"Revenue should be recognized when it is realizable and earned." —FASB

SEC additional guidance:

1. Evidence of an arrangement between buyer and seller

2. Completion of the earnings process, firm has delivered product or service

3. Price is determined

4. Assurance of payment, able to estimate probability of payment

© Kaplan, Inc.   8

Revenue Recognition Methods

Sales-basis method—used when good or service is provided at time of sale, cash, or credit with high payment probability (majority of transactions)

Exceptions (construction contracts)

1. Percentage-of-completion method—used for L-T projects under contract, with **reliable estimates** of revenues, costs, and completion time

© Kaplan, Inc.   9

Revenue Recognition Methods

2. Completed-contract method (U.S. GAAP)— used for L-T projects with no contract, or unreliable estimates of revenue or costs; revenue and expenses are not recognized until **project is completed**
IFRS: Report revenue but no profit

Both U.S. GAAP and IFRS: If a loss on the overall contract is estimated during any period, the loss must be recognized in that period under POC and CC methods.

© Kaplan, Inc.   10

Revenue Recognition Methods

Installment Sale: Payments for an asset purchase are made over an extended period.

Under IFRS

- Sale price is recorded as revenue at the time of sale; interest is recognized as revenue over the life of the contract.

  - Exception: Some real estate sales require deferral of revenue recognition.

  - If outcome cannot be reliably estimated, revenue recognition under IFRS is similar to cost recovery method (however, the term is not used).

© Kaplan, Inc.   11

LOS 24.b,c Describe/Calculate
CFAI p. 153, Schweser p. 41   Understanding Income Statements

Revenue Recognition Methods

Under U.S. GAAP

3. **Installment method** is used when firm cannot estimate likelihood of collection on an installment sale, but cost of goods/services is known; revenue and profit are based on percentage of cash collected.

4. **Cost recovery method (most extreme)** is used when cost of goods/services is unknown and firm cannot estimate the likelihood of collection; only recognize profit after all costs are recovered.

Use of these methods is rare, especially for sale of anything but real estate.

© Kaplan, Inc.   12

LOS 24.b,c Describe/Calculate
CFAI p. 153, Schweser p. 41   Understanding Income Statements

Percentage-of-Completion Method

Cumulative revenue

$$\frac{\text{Total costs to date}}{\text{Total project cost}} \times \text{Sales price} = \quad \text{X}$$

Revenue recognized in prior years	(X)
This period's revenue	X
Costs incurred in period	(X)
Profit recognized in period	X

Must do this calculation if total cost estimate changes

© Kaplan, Inc.   13

LOS 24.b,c Describe/Calculate
CFAI p. 153, Schweser p. 41   Understanding Income Statements

Percentage-of-Completion Method

Wildon Properties, Ltd., has a contract to build a hotel for $2,000,000 to be received in equal installments over 4 years.

A reliable estimate of total cost of this contract is $1,600,000.

During the first year, Wildon incurred $400,000 in cost. During the second year, $500,000 of costs were incurred and the estimate of total cost did not change.

Calculate the revenue and profit to be recognized in each of the first two years.

© Kaplan, Inc.   14

LOS 24.b,c Describe/Calculate
CFAI p. 153, Schweser p. 41   Understanding Income Statements

Percentage-of-Completion Method
Solution

Year 1: $2,000,000 × (400,000 / 1,600,000)

Revenue = $500,000

Profit = $500,000 − $400,000 = $100,000

Year 2: $2,000,000 × (900,000 / 1,600,000) − $500,000

Revenue = $625,000

Profit = $625,000 − $500,000 = $125,000

© Kaplan, Inc.   15 - 6

Completed-Contract Method

Revenue and expenses are not recognized until the **project is completed.**

Example: Building a hotel for $40 million, cost to build is $32 million; cost incurred in <u>Year 1</u> is $6.4 million

revenue = 0; expense = 0; income = 0

On completion/final year:
revenue = $40m; expenses = $32m; income = $8m

© Kaplan, Inc.

16

IFRS: Long-term Contracts With Uncertain Outcome

Revenue and expenses are recognized over the project's life; however, no profit is recorded until **project is completed** (similar to completed-contract).

Example: Building a hotel for €40 million, cost to build is €32 million; cost incurred in <u>Year 1</u> is €6.4 million

Revenue = 6.4m; expense = 6.4m; income = 0

On completion/final year:

Income = €8m

© Kaplan, Inc.

17

Cost Recovery Method – Example

During 20X0, Cook, Inc., sold $20,000 of services, but the cost of providing this service was unclear at the outset of the contract. During 20X0 and 20X1, Cook collected $8,000 and $12,000, respectively, of its receivables. The project was completed during 20X1, at which time the company had incurred total costs of $10,000.

Under the cost recovery method, what are the sales and gross profit to be reported in each of the two years?

© Kaplan, Inc.

18

Cost Recovery Method – Solution

	20X0	20X1
Sales	8,000	12,000
Cost of sales	(8,000)	(2,000)
Gross profit	0	10,000

© Kaplan, Inc.

19 - 3

LOS 24.b,c Describe/Calculate
CFAI p. 153, Schweser p. 41   Understanding Income Statements

Barter or Non-Monetary Exchanges

- Exchange of goods or services between two parties (no exchange of cash)
- A agrees to exchange inventory for a service provided by B
- **IFRS:** Revenue = fair value of similar non-barter transactions with unrelated parties
- **U.S. GAAP:** Revenue = fair value only if the company has received cash payments for such services historically (otherwise record sale at carrying value of asset)

© Kaplan, Inc.   20

LOS 24.b,c Describe/Calculate
CFAI p. 153, Schweser p. 41   Understanding Income Statements

Gross vs. Net Reporting

- Internet-based merchandising companies
- Sell product but never hold in inventory
- Arrangement for supplier to ship directly to end customer

	Gross Reporting		Sales commission
Revenue	100		$
Cost of good sold	80		
Gross profit	20		Net sale 20

© Kaplan, Inc.   21

LOS 24.b,c Describe/Calculate
CFAI p. 153, Schweser p. 41   Understanding Income Statements

Gross vs. Net Reporting

U.S. GAAP: Report gross if company:

- Is primary obligator
- Bears inventory risk
- Bears credit risk
- Can choose supplier
- Has latitude to set price

If criteria are not met, then company is acting as an agent: report net

© Kaplan, Inc.   22

LOS 24.b,c Describe/Calculate
CFAI p. 153, Schweser p. 41   Understanding Income Statements

Implications for Analysis

Review revenue recognition policies in footnotes:

- Earlier revenue recognition—aggressive
- Later revenue recognition—conservative
- Consider estimates used in methods
- Assess how different policies would affect financial ratios

© Kaplan, Inc.   23

Understanding Income Statements

Project cost estimate = $10 million; contract totals $12 million; $2 million of costs occur in each of Years 1 and 2; invoiced amounts $4 million in Year 1 and $3 million in Year 2; $1 million in cash collected each year. Year 2 income under percentage of completion is:

A. $1 million.

B. $400,000.

C. $1 million loss.

© Kaplan, Inc.

24 - 2

LOS 24.d Describe
CFAI p. 166, Schweser p. 47   **Understanding Income Statements**

IFRS–U.S. GAAP Convergence:
Revenue Recognition Standards

- Principles-based approach to revenue recognition
- New guidance issued May 2014
  - U.S. GAAP: Effective December 2017, may adopt for periods beginning December 2016
  - IFRS: Effective January 2018, may adopt early

© Kaplan, Inc.

25

LOS 24.d Describe
CFAI p. 166, Schweser p. 47   **Understanding Income Statements**

IFRS–U.S. GAAP Convergence:
Revenue Recognition Standards

New five-step model for revenue recognition:

1. Identify **contracts** with customer
2. Identify **performance obligations** in contracts
3. Determine **transaction price**
4. Allocate transaction price to performance obligations
5. Recognize revenue when/as performance obligations are satisfied

© Kaplan, Inc.

26

LOS 24.d Describe
CFAI p. 166, Schweser p. 47   **Understanding Income Statements**

IFRS–U.S. GAAP Convergence:
Revenue Recognition Standards

New disclosure requirements:

- Contracts with customers, disaggregated into categories
- Contract-related assets and liabilities:
  - Balances and changes
  - Remaining performance obligations, transaction prices allocated to them
  - Significant judgments, changes in judgments

© Kaplan, Inc.

27

LOS 24.e Describe
CFAI p. 170, Schweser p. 48   Understanding Income Statements

Expense Recognition

<u>Accrual basis—matching principle</u>

Match costs against associated revenues

Examples:

- Inventory (COGS)
- Depreciation/amortization
- Warranty expense
- Doubtful debt expense

<u>Period expenses</u>

Expenditures that less directly match the timing of revenues (e.g., administrative costs)

© Kaplan, Inc.   28

LOS 24.e Describe
CFAI p. 170, Schweser p. 48   Understanding Income Statements

Analysis Implications

- Inventory valuation
- Warranty expense
- Depreciation
- Amortization
- Doubtful debt provisions
- Revenue recognition

> All require significant estimates and assumptions affecting net income.

- Review year-on-year consistency
- Review footnotes and MD&A

© Kaplan, Inc.   29

LOS 24.e Describe
CFAI p. 170, Schweser p. 48   Understanding Income Statements

Amortization

- Amortization of intangible assets (e.g., patents)
- Spreading cost over life
- If the earnings pattern cannot be established, use straight line (IAS 38)
- IFRS and U.S. GAAP firms both typically amortize straight-line with no residual value
- Goodwill not amortized—checked annually for impairment

© Kaplan, Inc.   30

LOS 24.f Describe
CFAI p. 179, Schweser p. 54   Understanding Income Statements

Unusual or Infrequent Items

Reported pretax before net income from continuing operations (above the line)

Unusual or infrequent Items may include:

- Gain (loss) from disposal of a *business segment or assets*
- Gain (loss) from sale of investment in subsidiary
- Provisions for environmental remediation
- Impairments, write-offs, write-downs, restructuring
- Integration expense for recently acquired business

"Extraordinary items" (unusual *and* infrequent) are no longer recognized as a separate category

© Kaplan, Inc.   31

LOS 24.f Describe
CFAI p. 179, Schweser p. 54   **Understanding Income Statements**

Discontinued Operations

Operations that management has decided to dispose of but (1) has not done so yet or (2) did so in current year after it generated profit or loss

Reported net of taxes after net income from continuing operations (below the line)

Assets, operations, and financing activities must be physically and operationally distinct from firm.

© Kaplan, Inc.

32

LOS 24.f Describe
CFAI p. 179, Schweser p. 54   **Understanding Income Statements**

Accounting Changes

Two types of accounting changes:

1. Change in accounting principle (e.g., inventory cost method)

   Retrospective application: IFRS and U.S. GAAP require prior years' data shown in the financial statements to be adjusted.

© Kaplan, Inc.

33

LOS 24.f Describe
CFAI p. 179, Schweser p. 54   **Understanding Income Statements**

Accounting Changes

2. Change in accounting estimate (e.g., change in depreciation method or useful life, salvage value)

   ▪ Does not require restatement of prior period earnings

   ▪ Disclosed in footnotes

   ▪ Typically, changes do not affect cash flow

© Kaplan, Inc.

34

LOS 24.f Describe
CFAI p. 179, Schweser p. 54   **Understanding Income Statements**

Accounting Changes

Prior period adjustments

Correcting errors or changing from an incorrect accounting method to one that is acceptable under GAAP

Typically requires restatement of prior period financial statements

Must **disclose** the nature of the error and its effect on net income

© Kaplan, Inc.

35

Non-Operating Items

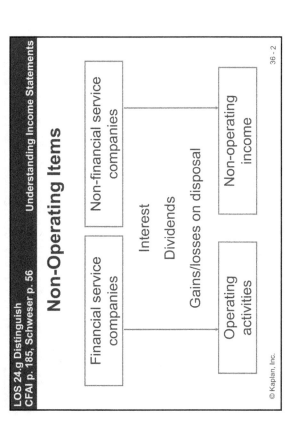

Financial service companies

Non-financial service companies

Interest

Dividends

Gains/losses on disposal

Operating activities

Non-operating income

Simple vs. Complex Capital Structures

A **simple capital structure** contains no *potentially* dilutive securities.

  Firm reports only basic EPS.

A **complex capital structure** contains *potentially* dilutive securities.

  Firm must report both basic and diluted EPS.

Dilutive vs. Antidilutive Securities

Potentially dilutive securities:

- Stock options
- Warrants
- Convertible debt
- Convertible preferred stock

Dilutive securities decrease EPS if exercised or converted to common stock.

Antidilutive securities increase EPS if exercised or converted to common stock.

Calculating Basic EPS

$$\text{Basic EPS} = \frac{\text{Net income} - \text{preferred dividends}}{\text{Weighted average \# common stock}}$$

- Net income minus preferred dividends equals earnings available to common stockholders
- Note that common stock dividends are not subtracted from net income

Stock Dividends and Stock Splits

- A 10% stock dividend increases shares outstanding by 10%.

- A 2-for-1 stock split increases shares outstanding by 100%.

- In calculating the weighted average shares outstanding, stock dividends and splits are applied retroactively to the beginning of the year, or the stock's issue date for new stock.

- Although weighted average shares are actually based on days, the exam is likely to use months.

© Kaplan, Inc.

40

Calculating the Weighted-Average Number of Shares Outstanding

1/1/X3	Shares outstanding	10,000
4/1/X3	Shares issued	4,000
7/1/X3	10% stock dividend	
9/1/X3	Shares repurchased	3,000

Shares adjusted for the 10% dividend:

1/1/X3	Initial shares (× 1.1)	11,000
4/1/X3	Shared issued (× 1.1)	4,400
9/1/X3	Shares repurchased (no adj.)	3,000

© Kaplan, Inc.

41 - 3

Calculating the Weighted-Average Number of Shares Outstanding

Initial shares (11,000) (12 months)	132,000
Shares issued (4,400) (9 months)	39,600
Shares repurchased (3,000) (4 months)	(12,000)
Total weighted shares	159,600
Weighted average shares outstanding 159,600 / 12	13,300

© Kaplan, Inc.

42 - 5

Diluted Earnings Per Share

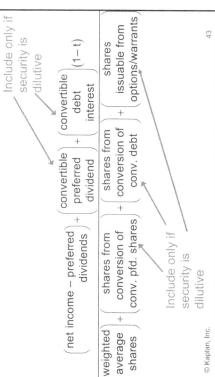

Include only if
security is
dilutive

Include only if
security is
dilutive

© Kaplan, Inc.

43

Checking for Dilution

- Only those securities that **would reduce EPS** below basic EPS if converted are used in the calculation of diluted EPS.

<u>Conv. pfd</u>: is dividends/new shares < basic?

<u>Conv. debt</u>: is interest (1 − t) / new shares < basic?

<u>Options and warrants</u>: is avg. price > ex. price?

If answer is **yes**, the security is **dilutive**.

© Kaplan, Inc.

44

Convertible Preferred Stock – Example

Earnings available to common,
year to 12/31/X1 $4,000,000
Common stock   2,000,000 sh.
Basic EPS $2.00

$5,000,000 of 7% convertible preferred stock is outstanding all year. The terms of conversion are that every $10 nominal value of preferred stock can be converted to 1.1 common shares.

Calculate fully diluted EPS for 20X1.

© Kaplan, Inc.

45

Convertible Preferred Stock – Example

	$
Earnings available to common	4,000,000
Add: Preferred dividend saved	350,000
	4,350,000

No. of common stock shares if preferred shares were converted:

Outstanding all year	2,000,000
On conversion $5,000,000 / 10 × 1.1	550,000
	2,550,000

© Kaplan, Inc.

46 - 2

Convertible Preferred Stock – Example

Check for dilution:

$$\frac{\text{Preferred Dividend}}{\text{Shares Created}} \quad < \quad \text{Basic EPS?}$$

$$\frac{\$350,000}{550,000} \quad < \quad \$2.00$$

Diluted EPS:

$$\frac{\$4,350,000}{2,550,000} = \$1.71$$

© Kaplan, Inc.

47 - 2

LOS 24.h,i Describe/Calculate/Interpret/Distinguish
CFAI p. 186, Schweser p. 56   **Understanding Income Statements**

Convertible Bonds – Example

Earnings available to common, year to 12/31/X1 $2,500,000
Common stock   1,000,000 sh.
Basic EPS $2.50
Tax rate   30%

$2,000,000 par value of 5% convertible bonds have been outstanding all year. Each $1,000 par value convertible bond can be converted to 120 common shares.

Calculate fully diluted EPS for 20X1.

© Kaplan, Inc.   48

LOS 24.h,i Describe/Calculate/Interpret/Distinguish
CFAI p. 186, Schweser p. 56   **Understanding Income Statements**

Convertible Bonds – Example

	$	$
Earnings available to common		2,500,000
Add: Interest saved	100,000	
Less: Tax @ 30%	(30,000)	
		70,000
		2,570,000

No. of common shares if bonds were converted:
Outstanding		1,000,000
On conversion $2,000,000 / $1,000 × 120		240,000
		1,240,000

© Kaplan, Inc.   49 - 3

LOS 24.h,i Describe/Calculate/Interpret/Distinguish
CFAI p. 186, Schweser p. 56   **Understanding Income Statements**

Convertible Bonds – Solution

Check for dilution:

$$\frac{\text{Interest savings } (1-t)}{\text{Shares created}} \;<\; \text{Basic EPS?}$$

$$\frac{\$70,000}{240,000} \;<\; \$2.50$$

Diluted EPS:

$$\frac{\$2,570,000}{1,240,000} = \$2.07$$

© Kaplan, Inc.   50 - 2

LOS 24.h,i Describe/Calculate/Interpret/Distinguish
CFAI p. 186, Schweser p. 56   **Understanding Income Statements**

Dilutive Stock Options – Treasury Stock Method

Dilutive only when the exercise price is less than the average market price

STEPS

1. Calculate number of common shares created if options are exercised

2. Calculate cash received from exercise

3. Calculate number of shares that can be purchased at the average market price with exercise proceeds

4. Calculate net increase in common shares outstanding

© Kaplan, Inc.   51

LOS 24.h,i Describe/Calculate/Interpret/Distinguish
CFAI p. 186, Schweser p. 56   Understanding Income Statements

Dilutive Employee Stock Options— Example

Earnings for equity in year to 31/Dec/X1	$1,200,000
Weighted average no. of common stock shares	500,000
Average price of common stock during year	$20
Exercise price	$15
Number of options outstanding in the year	100,000
Basic EPS	**$2.40**

Calculate diluted EPS for 20X1.

© Kaplan, Inc.

52

LOS 24.h,i Describe/Calculate/Interpret/Distinguish
CFAI p. 186, Schweser p. 56   Understanding Income Statements

Dilutive Stock Options – Example

Step 1 – Assume all options are exercised
Shares issued = 100,000

Step 2 – Calculate cash proceeds
Proceeds if all options exercised: 100,000 × $15 = $1,500,000

Step 3 – Calculate number of shares that can be bought at average price

$$\frac{\$1,500,000}{\$20} = 75,000 \text{ shares}$$

Step 4 – Calculate net increase in common stock

Total shares needed	100,000
Shares "purchased" with proceeds	75,000
Number of new shares needed	25,000

© Kaplan, Inc.

53 - 4

LOS 24.h,i Describe/Calculate/Interpret/Distinguish
CFAI p. 186, Schweser p. 56   Understanding Income Statements

Dilutive Stock Options

Diluted EPS: $\dfrac{\$1,200,000}{525,000} = \$2.29$

© Kaplan, Inc.

54 - 1

LOS 24.j,k Convert/Evaluate
CFAI p. 195, Schweser p. 65   Understanding Income Statements

Vertical Common-Size Income Statements

$$\frac{\text{Income statement account}}{\text{Sales}} \quad e.g., \quad \frac{Marketing\ expense}{Sales}$$

- Converts income statement to relative percentages
- Useful for comparing entities of differing sizes
- Compare % to strategy in MD&A
- Time series or cross-section use
- Gross and net profit margin are common-size ratios

© Kaplan, Inc.

55

Understanding Income Statements

Jan 1   10,000 shares
Mar 1   3,000 shares issued
July 1   20% stock dividend
Nov 1   3,000 shares repurchased

The weighted average number of shares outstanding over the year equals:

A. 12,000.
B. 11,300.
C. 14,500.

© Kaplan, Inc.   57 - 2

LOS 25.a Describe
CFAI p. 212, Schweser p. 80   **Understanding Balance Sheets**

Components and Format of Balance Sheet

Balance Sheet	$m				$m
Current assets			**Current liabilities**		70
Cash	50		**Long-term liabilities**		180
Others	100	150			250
Long-lived assets			**Owners' equity**		
Investments	20		Contributed capital	100	
PP&E	200		Retained earnings	70	
Intangibles	50				170
Total assets		420	**Liabilities and equity**		420

© Kaplan, Inc.   59

LOS 24.l.m Describe/Calculate/Interpret/Identify
CFAI p. 199, Schweser p. 67   **Understanding Income Statements**

Comprehensive Income

Comprehensive income =
Net income + Other comprehensive income

Net income from income statement	X
Δ Foreign currency translation adjustment	X/(X)
Δ Minimum pension liability adjustment	X/(X)
Δ Unrealized gains or losses on derivatives contracts accounted for as hedges	X/(X)
Δ Unrealized gains and losses on available for sale securities	X/(X)
Comprehensive income	X

Other Comprehensive Income

© Kaplan, Inc.   56

Financial Reporting and Analysis

Income Statements, Balance Sheets, and Cash Flow Statements

25. Understanding Balance Sheets

LOS 25.a Describe
CFAI p. 212, Schweser p. 80

Assets

Asset recognition:

- Probable future flow of future economic benefit to the entity
- Measurable with reliability

Cash and equivalents

Inventories

Trade and other receivables

Prepaid expenses

Financial assets

Deferred tax assets

Property, plant, and equipment

Investment property

Intangible assets

Equity a/c investments

Natural resources

Assets held for sale

Assets Disclosed on the B/S

© Kaplan, Inc.

60

LOS 25.a Describe
CFAI p. 212, Schweser p. 80

Liabilities

Liability recognition:

- Probable sacrifice of future economic benefit to the entity as a result of past transactions/events
- Amounts received but not reported as revenue in the income statement (deferred/unearned revenue)
- Amounts reported as expenses but which have not been paid

Bank borrowings

Notes payable

Provisions

Unearned revenues

Accounts payable

Financial liabilities

Accrued liabilities

Deferred tax liabilities

Liabilities Disclosed on the B/S

© Kaplan, Inc.

61

LOS 25.a Describe
CFAI p. 212, Schweser p. 80

Equity

Assets − Liabilities = Equity

Net Assets

Capital Characteristics

Permanent

No mandatory charges against earnings

Legal subordination to creditors

© Kaplan, Inc.

62

LOS 25.b Describe
CFAI p. 212, Schweser p. 81

Balance Sheet Analysis

Use balance sheet analysis to assess liquidity, solvency, and ability to make distributions to shareholders

Limitations

- Mixed measurement conventions:
  - Historic cost
  - Amortized cost
  - Fair value
- Fair values may change after balance sheet date
- Off-balance-sheet assets and liabilities

© Kaplan, Inc.

63

LOS 25.c Describe
CFAI p. 215, Schweser p. 81   Understanding Balance Sheets

Balance Sheet Format

Report format

Assets, liabilities, and equity in a single column

Account format

Assets on the left

Liabilities and equity on the right

Classified balance sheet

Grouping of accounts into sub-categories:

- Current vs. non-current
- Financial vs. non-financial

Liquidity-based presentation (financial institutions)

© Kaplan, Inc.   64

LOS 25.d,e Distinguish/Describe
CFAI p. 217, Schweser p. 81   Understanding Balance Sheets

Current Assets

Current assets include cash and other assets that will likely be converted into cash or used up within one year or one operating cycle, whichever is greater.

The **operating cycle** is the time it takes to produce or purchase inventory, sell the product, and collect the cash.

Current assets are presented in the order of liquidity.

Current assets reveal information about the operating activities/capacity of the firm.

© Kaplan, Inc.   65

LOS 25.d,e Distinguish/Describe
CFAI p. 217, Schweser p. 81   Understanding Balance Sheets

Current Assets

Cash and cash equivalents: amortized cost or fair value

Marketable securities: amortized cost or fair value

Accounts receivable/trade receivables: net realizable value

Inventories:

- Raw materials, work in process, finished goods
- Manufacturing (standardized costs)
- Cost flow methodology (FIFO, Avco, LIFO)

Prepaid expenses: historic cost

Deferred tax assets: net of valuation allowance

© Kaplan, Inc.   66

LOS 25.d,e Distinguish/Describe
CFAI p. 217, Schweser p. 81   Understanding Balance Sheets

Noncurrent Assets

Assets held for continuing use within the business, not resale

Assets not consumed or disposed of in the current period

Represent the infrastructure from which the entity operates

Provides information on the firm's investing activities

© Kaplan, Inc.   67

Accounting for Long-Term Assets

Long-term assets convey benefits over time.

Tangible assets (e.g., land, buildings, equipment, natural resources)

Intangible assets (e.g., copyrights, patents, trademarks, franchises, and goodwill)

Investment property (IFRS only)—generates investment income or capital appreciation

Plant, property, and equipment recorded at purchase cost, including shipping and installation, or construction cost including labor, materials, overhead, and interest

© Kaplan, Inc.   68

Goodwill

Goodwill is the difference between acquisition price and the fair market value of the acquired firm's net assets.

The additional amount paid represents the amount paid for assets not recorded on the balance sheet.

Acquisition price	$
FMV net assets acquired	(X)
Goodwill	X

Fair value involves management discretion—goodwill is not amortized!

© Kaplan, Inc.   69

Goodwill Analysis

Impairment indicates that goodwill often results from overpayment to acquire entity.

Remove the impact of goodwill from ratios:

- Remove goodwill from assets
- Remove any impairment from income statement
- Evaluate business acquisitions considering:
    - Purchase price
    - Net assets
    - Earnings prospects

© Kaplan, Inc.   70

Financial Assets/Liabilities

Stocks   Bonds

Receivables   Notes receivable

Notes payable   Loans

Derivatives

© Kaplan, Inc.   71

Slide 72

Fair Value Assets and Liabilities

Financial assets
- Trading securities
- Available-for-sale securities
- Derivatives (standalone or embedded in a non-derivative instrument)
- Assets with fair value exposures hedged by derivatives

Financial liabilities
- Derivatives
- Non-derivative investments with fair value exposures hedged by derivatives

© Kaplan, Inc.

72

Slide 73

Cost or Amortized Cost

Financial assets
- Unlisted instruments
- Held-to-maturity investments
- Loans
- Receivables

Financial liabilities
All other liabilities (e.g., bonds, notes payable, etc.)

© Kaplan, Inc.

73

Slide 74

Marketable Securities

Classification of securities based on company's intent with regard to eventual sale:

Held-to-maturity securities
- Debt securities that the company intends to hold to maturity
- Securities are carried at cost
- I/S income and realized gains/(losses) on disposal

Available-for-sale securities
- May be sold to satisfy company needs
- Debt or equity
- Current or non-current
- Carried on balance sheet at market value
- Income statement same as HTM method

© Kaplan, Inc.

74

Slide 75

Marketable Securities

Trading securities
- Acquired for the purpose of selling in the near term
- Carried on the balance sheet as current assets at market value
- Income statement includes dividends, realized and unrealized gains/losses

© Kaplan, Inc.

75

Marketable Securities

Type of Security	Held to maturity	Available for sale	Trading
Interest income	Income statement	Income statement	Income statement
Unrealized G/L	Carried at cost	OCI to BS	Income statement
Realized G/L	Income statement	Income statement	Income statement

© Kaplan, Inc.

76

Current Liabilities

Satisfies any of the following four criteria:

1. Expected to be settled in the entity's normal operating cycle

2. Held primarily for the purpose of being traded

3. Is due to be settled < 12 months from the balance sheet date

4. The entity does not have a right to defer settlement for > 12 months

All other liabilities are noncurrent.

© Kaplan, Inc.

77

Current Liabilities

- Accounts payable/trade payables
- Notes payable
- Current portion of long-term debt
- Accrued liabilities
- Taxes payable
- Unearned revenue

© Kaplan, Inc.

78

For financial assets classified as available for sale, how are unrealized gains and losses reflected in shareholders' equity?

A. They are not recognized.

B. They flow through retained earnings.

C. They are a component of accumulated other comprehensive income.

79 - 1

LOS 25.f Describe
CFAI p. 241, Schweser p. 90 — Understanding Balance Sheets

Components of Equity

- Capital contributed by owners

  Also termed *common stock or issued capital*

- Preferred stock (not redeemable)

- Treasury stock (reduces equity)

- Retained earnings

- Noncontrolling (minority) interest

- Accumulated other comprehensive income

© Kaplan, Inc.

80

LOS 25.f Describe
CFAI p. 241, Schweser p. 90 — Understanding Balance Sheets

Statement of Changes in Stockholders' Equity

	Common Stock	Retained Earnings (in thousands)	Accumulated Other Comprehensive Income (loss)	Total
Beginning balance	$49,234	$26,664	($406)	$75,492
Net income		6,994		6,994
Net unrealized loss on available-for-sale securities			(40)	(40)
Net unrealized loss on cash flow hedges			(56)	(56)
Adjustments to net pension liability			(26)	(26)
Cumulative translation adjustment			42	42
Comprehensive income				6,914
Issuance of common stock	1,282			1,282
Repurchases of common stock	(6,200)			(6,200)
Dividends		(2,360)		(2,360)
Ending balance	$44,316	$31,298	($486)	$75,128

OCI

© Kaplan, Inc.

81

LOS 25.g Convert/Interpret
CFAI p. 246, Schweser p. 92 — Understanding Balance Sheets

Common Size Balance Sheet

$$\frac{\text{Balance sheet account}}{\text{Total assets}} \quad e.g., \quad \frac{Inventory}{Total\ assets}$$

Uses:

Comparisons over time (trend analysis)

Cross-sectional comparisons

© Kaplan, Inc.

82

LOS 25.h Calculate/Interpret
CFAI p. 254, Schweser p. 94 — Understanding Balance Sheets

Liquidity Ratios

Current ratio
$$\frac{\text{Current assets}}{\text{Current liabilities}}$$

Quick ratio
$$\frac{\text{Current assets} - \text{inventory}}{\text{Current liabilities}}$$

Cash ratio
$$\frac{\text{Cash} + \text{marketable securities}}{\text{Current liabilities}}$$

© Kaplan, Inc.

83

LOS 25.h Calculate/Interpret
CFAI p. 254, Schweser p. 94

Income Statements, Balance Sheets, and Cash Flow Statements

26. Understanding Cash Flow Statements

KAPLAN UNIVERSITY SCHOOL OF PROFESSIONAL AND CONTINUING EDUCATION | SCHWESER

LOS 25.h Calculate/Interpret
CFAI p. 254, Schweser p. 94

Solvency Ratios

Long-term debt to equity $\dfrac{\text{Total long-term debt}}{\text{Total equity}}$

Debt to equity $\dfrac{\text{Total debt}}{\text{Total equity}}$

Total debt $\dfrac{\text{Total debt}}{\text{Total assets}}$

Financial leverage $\dfrac{\text{Total assets}}{\text{Total equity}}$

© Kaplan, Inc.

84

LOS 26.a Compare/Classify
CFAI p. 267, Schweser p. 103

Importance of Cash Flow Statement

Net income from accrual accounting does not tell us about the **sources and uses of cash** to meet liabilities and operating needs.

The statement of cash flows has **three components** under both IFRS and U.S. GAAP:

Cash provided or used by **operating** activities

Cash provided or used by **investing** activities

Cash provided or used in **financing** activities

© Kaplan, Inc.

86

LOS 26.a Compare/Classify
CFAI p. 267, Schweser p. 103

Operating Cash Flows (CFO)

	$
Cash received from customers	X
Cash dividends received	X
Cash interest received	X
Other cash income	X
Payments to suppliers	(X)
Cash expenses (wages, etc.)	(X)
Cash interest paid	(X)
Cash taxes paid	(X)
CFO	X/(X)

© Kaplan, Inc.

87

Investing Cash Flows (CFI)

- Purchases of property, plant, and equipment

- Proceeds from sales of assets

- Investments in joint ventures and affiliates

- Payments for businesses acquired

- Purchases and sales of intangibles

- Purchases or sales of marketable securities

- Excludes:

  - Trading securities (part of CFO)

    - Cash equivalents (part of balance sheet cash)

© Kaplan, Inc.

88

Financing Cash Flows

- Common stock issuance

- Treasury stock repurchases

- Preferred stock issuance and redemption

- Debt issuance and redemption

- Dividend payments (dividends rec'd CFO—U.S. GAAP)

Excludes indirect financing via accounts payable (CFO)

© Kaplan, Inc.

89

Non-Cash Investing and Financing Activities

Several types of transactions do not involve the payment or receipt of cash and are not reflected in financing and investing cash flows but are disclosed in the footnotes or other schedules.

Non-cash financing and investing activities:

- Converting debt or preferred into common equity

- Assets acquired under capital leases

- Purchase of assets via issuance of debt/equity

- Exchanging one non-cash asset for another

- Stock dividends

© Kaplan, Inc.

90

U.S. GAAP vs. IFRS

	U.S. GAAP	IFRS
Interest received	CFO	CFO or CFI
Interest paid	CFO	CFO or CFF
Dividends received	CFO	CFO or CFI
Dividends paid	CFF	CFO or CFF
Taxes paid	CFO	CFO or CFI & CFF
Bank overdraft	CFF	Considered part of cash and cash equivalents

© Kaplan, Inc.

91

Statement of Cash Flow:
Direct vs. Indirect Method

Direct versus indirect method refers only to the calculation of CFO; the value of CFO is the same for both methods; CFI and CFF are unaffected.

Direct method: Identify actual cash inflows and outflows (e.g., collections from customers, amounts paid to suppliers)

Indirect method: Begin with net income and make necessary adjustments to get operating cash flow

© Kaplan, Inc.

92

Linkages Between Statements

	Accounts Receivable 'T' Account		
Last year's balance sheet			This year's CF statement
AR B/Fwd	18,000		
Sales	200,000	198,000	Cash collections
		20,000	AR C/Fwd
This year's income statement	218,000	218,000	This year's balance sheet

© Kaplan, Inc.

93 - 5

Cash Inflows and Outflows

General rules regarding increases and decreases in balance sheet items over time:

	Increase	Decrease
Assets	outflow	inflow
Liabilities & Equity	inflow	outflow

e.g.: An increase in AR or inventory uses cash.
An increase in payables generates cash.
Adjust net income for these changes (indirect).

© Kaplan, Inc.

94

Ecclestone Industries—Example

Ecclestone Industries has the following income statement for 20X9 and balance sheets for 20X8 and 20X9. You are to construct the statement of cash flows using the **indirect method**.

Additional information:
Equipment was purchased for $50,000

© Kaplan, Inc.

95

Slide 96

Income Statement for Year to 31 December 20X9

	$	$
Sales revenue		200,000
Expenses:		
Cost of goods sold	80,000	
Salaries	10,000	
Depreciation	14,000	
Interest	1,000	
		105,000
		95,000
Gain from sale of PPE		20,000
Pre-tax income		115,000
Provision for taxes		40,000
Net income		75,000

© Kaplan, Inc.

96

Slide 97

Ecclestone Balance Sheet Data

Balance Sheets	20X8 $	20X9 $
Current assets		
Cash	18,000	66,000
Accounts receivable	18,000	20,000
Inventory	14,000	10,000
Non-current assets		
Gross PPE	282,000	312,000
Accum. Depr.	(80,000)	(84,000)
Total Assets	252,000	324,000

© Kaplan, Inc.

97

Slide 98

Balance Sheets	20X8 $	20X9 $
Current liabilities		
Accounts payable	10,000	18,000
Salaries payable	16,000	9,000
Interest payable	6,000	7,000
Taxes payable	8,000	10,000
Dividends payable	2,000	12,000
Noncurrent liabilities		
Bonds	20,000	30,000
Deferred taxes	30,000	40,000
Stockholders' equity		
Common stock	100,000	80,000
Retained earnings	60,000	118,000
Total Liabilities & Equity	252,000	324,000

© Kaplan, Inc.

98

Slide 99

Indirect Method CFO

Steps

1. Start with net income
2. Adjust net income for changes in relevant balance sheet items:

> Increases in an asset: deduct
> Increase in a liability: add
> Decrease in an asset: add
> Decrease in a liability: deduct

© Kaplan, Inc.

99

Indirect Method (continued)

3. Eliminate depreciation and amortization by adding them back (they've been deducted in arriving at net income but are non-cash expenses)

4. Eliminate gains on disposal by deducting them and losses on disposal by adding them back (these are CFI, not CFO)

© Kaplan, Inc.

100

Indirect Method Solution

	$
Net income	75,000
Add: Depreciation	14,000
Less: Gain from sale of PPE	(20,000)
Add: Increase in deferred taxes	10,000
Current asset adjustments	
Less: Increase in accounts receivable	(2,000)
Add: Decrease in inventory	4,000
Current liability adjustments	
Add: Increase in accounts payable	8,000
Less: Decrease in salaries payable	(7,000)
Add: Increase in interest payable	1,000
Add: Increase in taxes payable	2,000
Cash flow from operations	85,000

© Kaplan, Inc.

101 - 10

Calculating CFI

CFI = cash received on asset sales – asset purchases

From notes: Asset purchases = $50,000

Asset sales = NBV of asset sold + gain on sale

From income statement: Gain on sale = $20,000

Net book value = gross PPE – accum. depreciation

© Kaplan, Inc.

102

Ecclestone CFI

Gross Plant and Equip.		Accumulated Depreciation	
Beginning PPE	282,000	Begin Acc. Depr.	80,000
PPE purchased	+ 50,000	Depr. Expense	+ 14,000
Ending PPE	– 312,000	End Acc. Depr.	– 84,000
Cost of PPE sold	**20,000**	**Acc. Dep. of PPE sold**	**10,000**

Net Book Value of assets sold = 20,000 – 10,000 = **10,000**

Sales price of assets sold = 10,000 + 20,000 = **30,000**

CFI = $30,000 – $50,000 = –$20,000

© Kaplan, Inc.

103

Slide (104 - 5)

Last year Acme Corp. bought an asset for $72,000, depreciation expense was $15,000, accumulated depreciation increased by $5,000, and gross PPE increased by $32,000. If a gain on an asset sold during the year was $13,000, the sales proceeds on the asset sale were:

A. $30,000.

B. $43,000.

C. $48,000.

© Kaplan, Inc.

104 - 5

Slide (105)

Computing CFF

Change in debt

+ Change in common stock

− Cash dividends paid ──── Dividends declared

Financing Cash Flow + ΔDividends payable

Cash dividends paid

Net income

− Δ in retained earnings

Dividends declared

© Kaplan, Inc.

105

Slide (106)

Ecclestone CFF

Net income	75,000	Div. declared		17,000
− Δ in R/E	58,000	− Δ Div. payable		10,000
Div. Declared	17,000	**Cash div. paid**		**7,000**

Change in debt	+10,000
Decrease in common stock	−20,000
Cash dividends paid	−7,000
Cash flow from financing	**−17,000**

© Kaplan, Inc.

106

Slide (107 - 3)

Putting the Cash Flow Statement Together

	$
Cash flow from operations	85,000
Cash flow from investments	(20,000)
Cash flow from financing	(17,000)
Net increase in cash	48,000
Cash balance 12/31/X8	18,000
Cash balance 12/31/X9	66,000

© Kaplan, Inc.

107 - 3

Direct Method From Indirect CFO

1. Take each income statement item in turn (e.g., sales)

2. Move to the balance sheet and identify asset and liability accounts that relate to that income statement item—e.g., accounts receivable

3. Calculate the change in the balance sheet item during the period (ending balance – opening balance)

4. Apply the rule:

> Increases in an asset: deduct
> Increase in a liability: add
> Decrease in an asset: add
> Decrease in a liability: deduct

© Kaplan, Inc.

109

Direct From Indirect CFO

9. Keep moving down the income statement until all items included in net income have been addressed applying steps 1-8

10. Total up the amounts and you have CFO

© Kaplan, Inc.

111

Converting an Indirect Statement to a Direct Statement of Cash Flows

Most firms use the indirect method, but the analyst may want information on the cash flows by function; some examples of this technique are:

Net sales – Δ accounts receivable + Δ advances from customers = cash collections from customers

Cost of goods sold + Δ inventory – Δ accounts payable = cash paid for inputs (**COGS treated as positive number**)

Interest expense + Δ interest payable = cash interest

© Kaplan, Inc.

108

Direct From Indirect CFO

5. Adjust the income statement amount by the change in the balance sheet

6. Tick off the items dealt with in both the income statement and balance sheet

7. Move to the next item on the income statement and repeat

8. Ignore depreciation/amortization and gains/losses on the disposal of assets as these are non-cash or non-CFO items

© Kaplan, Inc.

110

Direct From Indirect CFO

Cash Inflows

Sales	200,000	
Less: Increase in A/R	(2,000)	
Cash collected from customers		198,000

Direct cash outflows

Cost of goods sold	(80,000)	
Add: Decrease in inventory	4,000	
Purchases	(76,000)	
Add: Increase in A/P	8,000	
Cash paid to suppliers		(68,000)
Operating expense (wages)	(10,000)	
Less: Decrease in salaries payable	(7,000)	
Cash paid to employees		(17,000)

© Kaplan, Inc.   112 - 6

Direct From Indirect CFO (continued)

Cash outflows

Interest Expense	(1,000)	
Add: Increase in interest payable	1,000	
Cash interest paid		0
Tax Expense	(40,000)	
Add: Increase in deferred tax liab.	10,000	
Tax payable	(30,000)	
Add: Increase in taxes payable	2,000	
Cash taxes paid		(28,000)
CFO		85,000

© Kaplan, Inc.   113 - 6

Cash Flow Statement Analysis

Benefits for the analyst

Do regular operations generate enough cash to sustain the business?

Is enough cash generated to pay off maturing debt?

Highlights the need for additional finance

Ability to meet unexpected obligations

The flexibility to take advantage of new business opportunities

© Kaplan, Inc.   114

Analysis

1. Analyze the major sources and uses of cash flow (CFO, CFI, CFF)
   - Where are the major sources and uses?
   - Is CFO positive and sufficient to cover capex?
2. Analyze CFO
   - What are the major determinants of CFO?
   - Is CFO higher or lower than NI?
   - How consistent is CFO?

© Kaplan, Inc.   115

Slide 116

LOS 26.h Analyze/Interpret
CFAI p. 294, Schweser p. 118

Understanding Cash Flow
Statements

Analysis

3. Analyze CFI
   - What is cash being spent on?
   - Is the company investing in PP&E?
   - What acquisitions have been made?
4. Analyze CFF
   - How is the company financing CFI and CFO?
   - Is the company raising or repaying capital?
   - What dividends are being returned to owners?

© Kaplan, Inc.

116

Slide 117

LOS 26.h Analyze/Interpret
CFAI p. 294, Schweser p. 118

Understanding Cash Flow
Statements

Common Size Statements

Two Approaches

Show each item as a
% of net revenue

Show each inflow as a
% of total inflows

Show each outflow as
a % of total outflows

Useful for:

Forecasting future cash
flows (% of net revenue)

Useful for:

Trend analysis
(time series)

© Kaplan, Inc.

117

Slide 118

LOS 26.h Analyze/Interpret
CFAI p. 294, Schweser p. 118

Understanding Cash Flow
Statements

Common Size Statements Ecclestone

Inflows

Receipts from customers	$198,000	83.2%
Sale of equipment	$30,000	12.6%
Debt issuance	$10,000	4.2%
Total	$238,000	100%

© Kaplan, Inc.

118

Slide 119

LOS 26.h Analyze/Interpret
CFAI p. 294, Schweser p. 118

Understanding Cash Flow
Statements

Common Size Statements Ecclestone

Outflows

Payments to suppliers	$68,000	35.8%
Payments to employees	$17,000	8.9%
Payments for interest	$ 0	0%
Payments for income tax	$28,000	14.7%
Purchase of equipment	$50,000	26.3%
Retirement of common stock	$20,000	10.5%
Dividend payments	$ 7,000	3.7%
Total	$190,000	100%

© Kaplan, Inc.

119

Free Cash Flow (FCF)

FCF is cash available for discretionary uses

Frequently used to value firms

$$FCFF = NI + NCC - WCInv + Int(1-T) - FCInv$$

$$FCFF = CFO + Int(1-T) - FCInv$$

$$FCFE = CFO - FCInv + Net debt increase$$

Free Cash Flow (FCF) Ecclestone

$$FCFF = CFO + Int(1-T) - FCInv$$

$$\$85,000 + \$1,000(1-0.4) - \$20,000 = \$65,600$$

$$FCFE = CFO - FCInv + Net debt increase$$

$$\$85,000 - \$20,000 + \$10,000 = \$75,000$$

$$FCFE = FCFF - Int(1-T) + Net debt increase$$

$$\$65,600 - \$1,000(1-0.4) + \$10,000 = \$75,000$$

Cash Flow Performance Ratios

$$Cash\ flow\ to\ revenue = \frac{CFO}{Net\ revenue}$$

$$Cash\ return\ on\ assets = \frac{CFO}{Avg\ total\ assets}$$

$$Cash\ return\ on\ equity = \frac{CFO}{Avg\ equity}$$

$$Cash\ to\ income = \frac{CFO}{Operating\ income}$$

Cash Flow Performance Ratios

$$Cash\ flow\ per\ share^* = \frac{CFO - pref\ div}{\#\ common\ stock}$$

*IFRS: If dividends paid were treated as CFO, they must be added back.

LOS 26.i Calculate/Interpret
CFAI p. 302, Schweser p. 120

Understanding Cash Flow Statements

Cash Flow Coverage Ratios

Debt coverage $\quad = \quad \dfrac{\text{CFO}}{\text{Total debt}}$

Interest coverage* $\quad = \quad \dfrac{\text{CFO} + \text{interest} + \text{tax}}{\text{Interest paid}}$

Reinvestment $\quad = \quad \dfrac{\text{CFO}}{\text{Cash paid for long-term assets}}$

*IFRS: If interest paid was treated as CFF, no addition is required.

© Kaplan, Inc.   124

LOS 26.i Calculate/Interpret
CFAI p. 302, Schweser p. 120

Understanding Cash Flow Statements

Cash Flow Coverage Ratios

Debt payment $\quad = \quad \dfrac{\text{CFO}}{\text{Cash paid for long-term debt repayment}}$

Dividend payment $\quad = \quad \dfrac{\text{CFO}}{\text{Dividends paid}}$

Investing and financing $\quad = \quad \dfrac{\text{CFO}}{\text{Cash outflows for CFI \& CFF}}$

© Kaplan, Inc.   125

Financial Reporting and Analysis

Income Statements, Balance Sheets, and Cash Flow Statements

27. Financial Analysis Techniques

KAPLAN UNIVERSITY SCHOOL OF PROFESSIONAL AND CONTINUING EDUCATION | **SCHWESER**

LOS 27.a Describe
CFAI p. 322, Schweser p. 137

Financial Analysis Techniques

Interpreting Ratios

1. Cross-sectional analysis:

   Comparison to industry norm or average

2. Time-series analysis (trend analysis):

   Comparison to a company's past ratios

Ratios help the analyst identify the questions that need further analysis.

© Kaplan, Inc.   127

Vertical Common-Size Statements

Income Statement

Income statement account e.g., Marketing expense

$$\frac{\text{Sales}}{\text{Sales}}$$

Balance Sheet

Balance sheet account   e.g., $\dfrac{\text{Inventory}}{\text{Total assets}}$

$$\frac{\text{Total assets}}{}$$

© Kaplan, Inc.

128

Horizontal Common-Size Statements

Each line shown as a relative to some base year

Facilitates trend analysis

Assets	Year 0	Year 1	Year 2
Cash	1.0	1.2	1.1
AR	1.0	1.3	1.0
Inventory	1.0	0.8	1.2
PP&E	1.0	1.5	2.0
Total	1.0	1.3	1.5

© Kaplan, Inc.

129

Common-Size Income Statement

Example: Consider a common-size income statement that reveals the following (selected items only):

Income Statement Item	20X7	20X8	Industry Avg.
COGS	58%	62%	60%
SG&A	18%	22%	18%
Net Income	9%	8%	10%

© Kaplan, Inc.

130

Limitations of Financial Ratios

Not useful in isolation – only valid when compared to other firms or the company's historical performance

Different accounting treatments – particularly when analyzing non-U.S. firms

Finding comparable industry ratios for companies that operate in multiple industries (homogeneity of operating activities)

All ratios must be viewed **relative** to one another

Determining the target or comparison value requires some **range of acceptable values**

© Kaplan, Inc.

131

Categories of Ratios

Activity ⟶ Efficiency of day-to-day tasks/operations

Liquidity ⟶ Ability to meet short-term liabilities

Solvency ⟶ Ability to meet long-term obligations

Profitability ⟶ Ability to generate profitable sales from asset base

Valuation ⟶ Quantity of asset or flow associated with an ownership claim

© Kaplan, Inc.

132

Ratio Analysis Context

1. Company goals and strategy
2. Industry norms
   - Ratios may be **industry specific**
   - **Multiple lines** of business distort aggregate ratios
     - Differences in **accounting methods**
     - Economic conditions

   Cyclical businesses and the **stage of the business cycle**

© Kaplan, Inc.

133

Ratio Analysis

Some general rules:

For ratios that use only **income statement items,** use the values from the current income statement

For ratios using only **balance sheet items,** use the values from the current balance sheet.

For ratios using **both income statement and balance sheet items,** use the value from the current income statement and the **average value for the balance sheet item.**

© Kaplan, Inc.

134

Activity Ratios

$$\text{Inventory turnover} = \frac{\text{Cost of goods sold}}{\text{Average inventory}}$$

$$\text{Days of inventory on hand (DOH)} = \frac{365}{\text{Inventory turnover}}$$

$$\text{Receivables turnover} = \frac{\text{Revenue}}{\text{Average receivables}}$$

$$\text{Days of sales outstanding (DSO)} = \frac{365}{\text{Receivables turnover}}$$

© Kaplan, Inc.

135

LOS 27.b Classify/Calculate/Interpret
CFAI p. 339, Schweser p. 143   **Financial Analysis Techniques**

Activity Ratios

Payables turnover $= \dfrac{\text{Purchases}}{\text{Average trade payables}}$

Number of days of payables $= \dfrac{365}{\text{Payables turnover}}$

Working capital turnover $= \dfrac{\text{Revenue}}{\text{Average working capital}}$

Working capital $=$ Current assets $-$ Current liabilities

© Kaplan, Inc.   136

LOS 27.b Classify/Calculate/Interpret
CFAI p. 339, Schweser p. 143   **Financial Analysis Techniques**

Activity Ratios

Fixed asset turnover $= \dfrac{\text{Revenue}}{\text{Average net fixed assets}}$ (Net of accumulated depreciation)

Total asset turnover $= \dfrac{\text{Revenue}}{\text{Average total assets}}$

© Kaplan, Inc.   137

LOS 27.b Classify/Calculate/Interpret
CFAI p. 339, Schweser p. 143   **Financial Analysis Techniques**

Definitions: Liquidity Ratios

Defensive interval ratio $= \dfrac{\text{Cash + short-term marketable investments + receivables}}{\text{Daily cash expenditure}}$

	Days
DOH	X
DSO	X
No. of days of payables	(X)
Cash conversion cycle	X

Cash conversion cycle =

© Kaplan, Inc.   138

LOS 27.b Classify/Calculate/Interpret
CFAI p. 339, Schweser p. 143   **Financial Analysis Techniques**

Cash Conversion Cycle

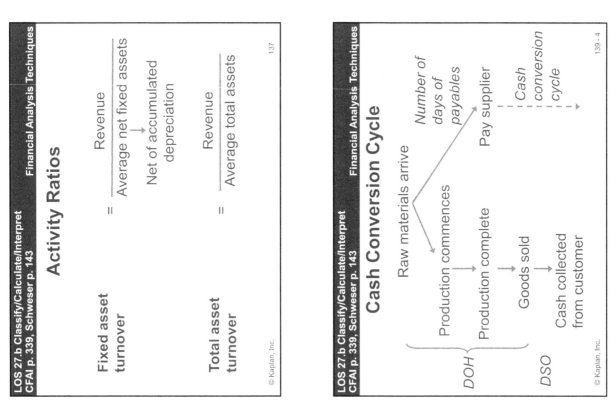

© Kaplan, Inc.   139 - 4

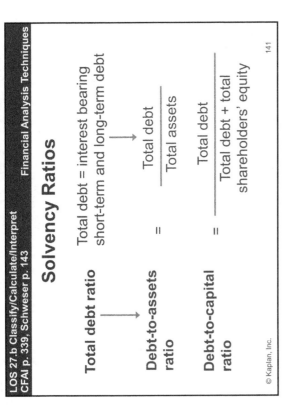

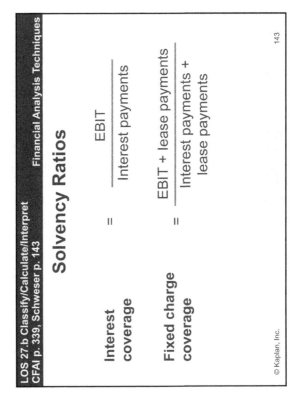

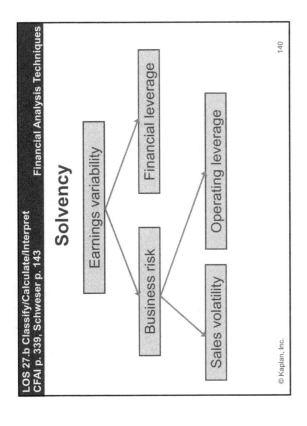

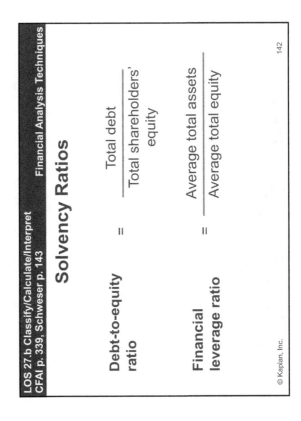

LOS 27.b Classify/Calculate/Interpret
CFAI p. 339, Schweser p. 143   **Financial Analysis Techniques**

Profitability Ratios

$$\text{Return on assets (ROA)} = \frac{\text{Net income}}{\text{Average total assets}}$$

Alternatively:

$$\text{Return on assets (ROA)} = \frac{\text{Net income} + \text{interest expense}\,(1-T)}{\text{Average total assets}}$$

$$\text{Operating ROA} = \frac{\text{Operating income}}{\text{Average total assets}}$$

© Kaplan, Inc.

144

LOS 27.b Classify/Calculate/Interpret
CFAI p. 339, Schweser p. 143   **Financial Analysis Techniques**

Profitability Ratios

$$\text{Return on total capital} = \frac{\text{EBIT}}{\text{Short- + long-term debt + equity}}$$

$$\text{Return on equity (ROE)} = \frac{\text{Net income}}{\text{Average total equity}}$$

$$\text{Return on common equity} = \frac{\text{Net income} - \text{pref. div.}}{\text{Average common equity}}$$

© Kaplan, Inc.

145

LOS 27.c Describe/Evaluate
CFAI p. 360, Schweser p. 152   **Financial Analysis Techniques**

Integrated Financial Ratio Approach

Important to **analyze** all ratios **collectively**

Use information from one ratio category to answer questions raised by another ratio

Classic example: **DuPont analysis**

© Kaplan, Inc.

146

LOS 27.c Describe/Evaluate
CFAI p. 360, Schweser p. 152   **Financial Analysis Techniques**

Integrated Financial Ratios – Example

	20X8	20X7	20X6
Current ratio	2.0	1.5	1.2
Quick ratio	0.5	0.8	1.0

	20X8	20X7	20X6
DOH	60	50	30
DSO	20	30	40

What can you conclude about this firm's performance? (Note that years are presented right-to-left.)

© Kaplan, Inc.

147

Integrated Financial Ratios – Example

1. Current ratio up – Quick ratio down – Why?

2. DOH has increased – indicates rising inventory rather than low cash

3. DSO decreasing – collecting cash from customers sooner

4. Current and quick ratios indicate the collected cash is being spent on inventory accumulation

5. Appears collections have been accelerated to make up for poor inventory management

DuPont System Analysis

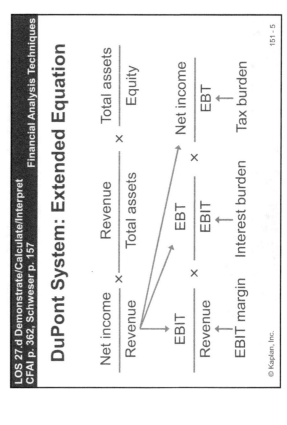

$$ROE = \frac{Net\ income}{Equity}$$

$$\frac{Net\ income}{Total\ assets} \quad\quad \times \quad\quad \frac{Total\ assets}{Equity}$$

ROA   Financial leverage ratio

DuPont System: Original Equation

$$ROE = \frac{Net\ income}{Equity}$$

$$\frac{Net\ income}{Revenue} \times \frac{Revenue}{Equity}$$

$$\frac{Net\ income}{Revenue} \times \frac{Revenue}{Total\ assets} \times \frac{Total\ assets}{Equity}$$

Net profit margin Asset turnover   Leverage

DuPont System: Extended Equation

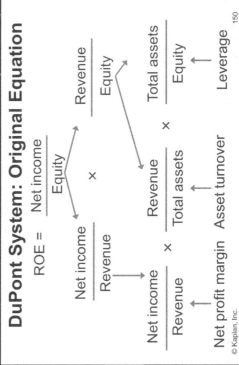

$$\frac{Net\ income}{Revenue} \times \frac{Revenue}{Total\ assets} \times \frac{Total\ assets}{Equity}$$

$$\frac{EBIT}{Revenue} \times \frac{EBT}{EBIT} \times \frac{Net\ income}{EBT}$$

EBIT margin Interest burden Tax burden

LOS 27.d Demonstrate/Calculate/Interpret
CFAI p. 362, Schweser p. 157   Financial Analysis Techniques

DuPont System: Extended Equation

$$\text{EBIT margin} \times \text{Interest burden} \times \text{Tax burden} \times \text{Asset turnover} \times \text{Leverage}$$

Operating profit margin

1 – Effective tax rate

© Kaplan, Inc.

152

LOS 27.e Calculate/Interpret
CFAI p. 368, Schweser p. 161   Financial Analysis Techniques

Per-Share Ratios for Valuation

$$\frac{P}{E} = \frac{\text{Price per share}}{\text{Earnings per share}}$$

$$\frac{P}{CF} = \frac{\text{Price per share}}{\text{Cash flow per share}}$$

$$\frac{P}{S} = \frac{\text{Price per share}}{\text{Sales per share}}$$

$$\frac{P}{BV} = \frac{\text{Price per Share}}{\text{Book value per share}}$$

© Kaplan, Inc.

153

LOS 27.e Calculate/Interpret
CFAI p. 368, Schweser p. 161   Financial Analysis Techniques

Per-Share Quantities

$$\text{Basic EPS} = \frac{\text{NI} - \text{Pref. div.}}{\text{Weighted avg. \# ordinary shares}}$$

$$\text{Diluted EPS} = \frac{\text{Income adjusted for dilutive securities}}{\text{Weighted avg. \# shares adjusted for dilution}}$$

$$\text{Cash flow per share} = \frac{\text{CFO}}{\text{Weighted avg. \# shares}}$$

© Kaplan, Inc.

154

LOS 27.e Calculate/Interpret
CFAI p. 368, Schweser p. 161   Financial Analysis Techniques

Per-Share Quantities

$$\text{EBITDA per share} = \frac{\text{EBITDA}}{\text{Avg. \# ordinary shares}}$$

$$\text{Dividends per share} = \frac{\text{Common dividend}}{\text{Weighted avg. \# common shares}}$$

© Kaplan, Inc.

155

Slide 156

Dividend Related Quantities

Dividend payout ratio $=$ $\dfrac{\text{Common dividend}}{\text{Net income} - \text{pref div}}$ → Net income available to common

Retention rate (b) $=$ $\dfrac{\text{Net income available to common} - \text{common dividends}}{\text{Net income attributable to common shares}}$

© Kaplan, Inc.

156

Slide 157

Dividend Related Quantities

Sustainable growth rate $=$ $b \times ROE$ ← Return on equity

Retention rate

$1 - \text{Dividend payout ratio}$

© Kaplan, Inc.

157

Slide 158-4

A firm has a dividend payout ratio of 35%, a net profit margin of 10%, an asset turnover of 1.4, and an equity multiplier leverage measure of 1.2. Estimate the firm's sustainable growth rate.

© Kaplan, Inc.

158 - 4

Slide 159

Business Risk Ratios

Coefficient of variation of operating income $=$ $\dfrac{\text{Std. dev. operating income}}{\text{Mean operating income}}$

Coefficient of variation of net income $=$ $\dfrac{\text{Std. dev. net income}}{\text{Mean net income}}$

Coefficient of variation of revenue $=$ $\dfrac{\text{Std. dev. revenue}}{\text{Mean revenue}}$

© Kaplan, Inc.

159

LOS 27.e Calculate/Interpret
CFAI p. 368, Schweser p. 161   **Financial Analysis Techniques**

Using Ratios for Equity Analysis

Research has found ratios (and changes in ratios) can be useful in forecasting earnings and stock returns (valuation).

Some items useful in forecasting:

% change in: current ratio • quick ratio • inventory • inventory turnover • inventory/total assets • sales • depreciation • capex/assets • asset turnover • depreciation/plant assets • total assets

ROE • Δ ROE • debt/equity • ROA • gross margin • working capital/assets • dividends/cash flow • Δ dividend • % debt repaid • operating ROA • pretax margin

© Kaplan, Inc.   160

LOS 27.e Calculate/Interpret
CFAI p. 368, Schweser p. 161   **Financial Analysis Techniques**

Credit Ratings and Ratios

Assessing a company's ability to service and repay its debt:

    Interest coverage ratio
    Return on capital   ┌─────────────────┐
    Debt-to-assets ratio   │ Also covered in │
    Other ratios focus on various measures of │ Fixed Income   │
    cash flow to total debt └─────────────────┘

Note: Adjustments are made for off-balance-sheet debt.

© Kaplan, Inc.   161

LOS 27.f Explain/Calculate/Interpret
CFAI p. 377, Schweser p. 165   **Financial Analysis Techniques**

Segment Reporting

Reportable business or geographic segment:

50% of its revenue from sales external to the firm, **and** at least 10% of a firm's revenue, earnings, or assets

- For each segment, firm reports *limited* financial statement information.

- For primary segments, must report revenue (internal and external), operating profit, assets, liabilities (IFRS only), capex, depreciation, and amortization.

© Kaplan, Inc.   162

LOS 27.f Explain/Calculate/Interpret
CFAI p. 377, Schweser p. 165   **Financial Analysis Techniques**

Definitions: Segment Ratios

$$\text{Segment (net)}\ \text{margin} = \frac{\text{Segment profit}}{\text{Segment revenue}}$$

$$\text{Segment asset}\ \text{turnover} = \frac{\text{Segment revenue}}{\text{Segment assets}}$$

$$\text{Segment ROA} = \frac{\text{Segment profit}}{\text{Segment assets}}$$

$$\text{Segment debt ratio}\ \text{(IFRS only)} = \frac{\text{Segment liabilities}}{\text{Segment assets}}$$

© Kaplan, Inc.   163

Model Building

■ Common-size statements and ratios can
  be used to model/forecast results

➢ Expected relationships among financial
  statement data

➢ Earnings model

➢ Revenue driven models

■ Sensitivity analysis

■ Scenario analysis

■ Simulation

Analysis has generated the following data:

Tax rate	35%
Equity multiplier	2.7
Net profit margin	4.6%
Equity turnover	5.2

ROE is *closest* to:

A. 13%

B. 17%

C. 24%

Additional Problems

1) Purple Fleur S.A., a retailer of floral products,
reported cost of goods sold for the year of $75
million. Total assets increased by $55 million, but
inventory declined by $6 million. Total liabilities
increased by $45 million, and accounts payable
increased by $2 million. The cash paid by the
company to its suppliers is most likely *closest* to:

A. $67 million.

B. $79 million.

C. $83 million.

CFA Curriculum Vol. 3,
R.24, Q.8, p. 206

2) During 2009, Argo Company sold 10 acres of prime commercial zoned land to a builder for $5,000,000. The builder gave Argo a $1,000,000 down payment and will pay the remaining balance of $4,000,000 to Argo in 2010. Argo purchased the land in 2002 for $2,000,000. Using the installment method, how much profit will Argo report for 2009?

A. $600,000.

B. $1,000,000.

C. $3,000,000.

-2-

CFA Curriculum Vol. 3,
R.25, Q.18, p. 260

3) Which of the following would an analyst *most likely* be able to determine from a common-size analysis of a company's balance sheet over several periods?

A. An increase or decrease in sales

B. An increase or decrease in financial leverage

C. A more efficient or less efficient use of assets

-1-

CFA Curriculum Vol. 3,
R.24, Q.12, p. 206

4) During 2009, Accent Toys, Plc., which began business in October of that year, purchased 10,000 units of a toy at a cost of £10 per unit in October. The toy sold well in October. In anticipation of heavy December sales, Accent purchased 5,000 additional units in November at a cost of £11 per unit. During 2009, Accent sold 12,000 units at a price of £15 per unit. Under the first in, first out (FIFO) method, what is Accent's cost of goods sold for 2009?

A. £120,000

B. £122,000

C. £124,000

-1-

Reading	Slide Number	Answer
24	24	B
24	57	C
25	79	C
26	104	B
27	158	10.92%
27	165	C

Additional Problems

1. A

2. A

3. B

4. B

Study Session 8

Financial Reporting and Analysis: Inventories, Long-Lived Assets, Income Taxes, and Non-Current Liabilities

Study Session 8   Financial Reporting and Analysis: Inventories, Long-Lived Assets, Income Taxes, and Non-Current Liabilities

172

Study Session 8

Inventories, Long-Lived Assets, Income Taxes, and Non-Current Liabilities

28. Inventories
29. Long-Lived Assets
30. Income Taxes
31. Non-Current (Long-Term) Liabilities

KAPLAN SCHOOL OF PROFESSIONAL | **SCHWESER**
UNIVERSITY AND CONTINUING EDUCATION

© Kaplan, Inc.

Inventories, Long-Lived Assets, Income Taxes, and Non-Current Liabilities

28. Inventories

KAPLAN SCHOOL OF PROFESSIONAL | **SCHWESER**
UNIVERSITY AND CONTINUING EDUCATION

LOS 28.a Distinguish
CFAI p. 397, Schweser p. 178

Inventory Equation

Beg. Inv + Purchases − COGS = End Inv

Or

Beg. Inv + Purchases − End Inv = COGS

	Matching Concept
Beginning inventory (BI)	X
Purchases (P)	X
Available for sale	X
Ending inventory (EI)	(X)
Cost of goods sold (COGS)	X

© Kaplan, Inc.

3

LOS 28.a Distinguish
CFAI p. 397, Schweser p. 178

Inventory Costs

Costs included in inventory (capitalized)

- Purchase cost net of discounts and rebates
- Transportation costs including insurance
- Conversion costs including labor and overhead
- Other costs "necessary to bring the inventory to its present location and condition"
- Any costs for storage required during the production process

© Kaplan, Inc.

4

173

Study Session 8   Financial Reporting and Analysis: Inventories, Long-Lived Assets, Income Taxes, and Non-Current Liabilities

Inventory Costs

Costs expensed as incurred

- Costs of any production inputs from abnormal waste

- Storage costs for finished goods

- Selling and administrative costs

Capitalization of Inventory Cost – Example

Units produced	1,500,000
Raw materials	$10,000,000
Direct labor	$5,300,000
Manufacturing overhead	$2,700,000
Freight-in to plant	$150,000
Storage cost of finished goods	$375,000
Abnormal waste	$200,000
Selling and administrative costs	$190,000

Which costs are included in inventory?

Capitalization of Inventory – Example

Materials	$10,000,000	
Labor cost	$5,300,000	} Conversion
Manufacturing overhead	$2,700,000	Cost
Freight-in to plant	$150,000	
Total capitalized cost	$18,150,000	
Units produced	1,500,000	
Cost per unit	$12.10	

Inventory Cost Flow Methods

		Assuming rising prices	
4 Methods	Description	Ending Inv.	COGS
FIFO	EI most recent purchases	Highest	Lowest
LIFO (U.S. GAAP)	EI oldest purchases	Lowest	Highest
AVCO	Average cost of units available	Middle	Middle
Specific Identification	Use cost of specific items		

174

Study Session 8   Financial Reporting and Analysis: Inventories, Long-Lived Assets, Income Taxes, and Non-Current Liabilities

LOS 28.c Calculate/Compare
CFAI p. 400, Schweser p. 180

Inventories

Example – Inventory Cost Flow

Assume beginning inventory consisted of two units costing $10 each. During the current period, three more units were purchased at $12 each, and then two units were purchased at $14 each. Three units were sold for $17 each.

Calculate COGS, gross profit, and ending inventory using FIFO, LIFO, and average cost.

© Kaplan, Inc.

9

LOS 28.c Calculate/Compare
CFAI p. 400, Schweser p. 180

Inventories

Example – Inventory Cost Flow

Unit purchase costs in order (sales of 3 units)

$10 $10 $12 $12 $12 $14 $14

First-in-first-out (FIFO)

Ending Inventory = $52

COGS = $32

Gross Profit = 3 × $17 – $32 = $19

© Kaplan, Inc.

10 - 3

LOS 28.c Calculate/Compare
CFAI p. 400, Schweser p. 180

Inventories

Example – Inventory Cost Flow

Unit purchase costs in order (sales of 3 units @ 17)

$10 $10 $12 $12 $12 $14 $14

Last-in-first-out (LIFO)

COGS = $40

Ending Inventory = $44

Gross Profit = 3 × $17 – $40 = $11

© Kaplan, Inc.

11 - 3

LOS 28.c Calculate/Compare
CFAI p. 400, Schweser p. 180

Inventories

Example – Inventory Cost Flow

Unit purchase costs in order (sales of 3 units)

$10 $10 $12 $12 $12 $14 $14

Average Cost = $12

Ending Inventory= 4 ×12 = $48   COGS = 3 ×12 = $36

Gross Profit = 3 ×17 – 36 = $15

© Kaplan, Inc.

12 - 4

175

Study Session 8   Financial Reporting and Analysis: Inventories, Long-Lived Assets, Income Taxes, and Non-Current Liabilities

Inventory Cost Flow and Price Changes

When prices are **rising** (as in the example):

1. FIFO provides an artificially low value of COGS and a better estimate of inventory.

2. LIFO provides an artificially low value of ending inventory and a better estimate of COGS.

When prices are declining, FIFO is still a better estimate of inventory and LIFO is still a better estimate of COGS.

With stable prices, all methods result in the same COGS, gross profit, and ending inventory.

© Kaplan, Inc.   13

Inventory Systems

Periodic System

- Inventory and COGS are determined at the end of the period

- Beg Inv + Purchases – End Inv = COGS

Perpetual System

- Inventory and COGS are continuously updated as each sale occurs

- Cannot use cost of inventory items not available at time of sale

© Kaplan, Inc.   14

Example – Inventory Systems

Use the following to calculate COGS and ending inventory under FIFO and LIFO for the month of March using a periodic and perpetual inventory system:

Mar 1 (beg. inventory)	4 units @ $3.00 per unit
Mar 14 sale	3 units
Mar 25 purchase	10 units @ $3.70 per unit
Mar 28 sale	8 units

© Kaplan, Inc.   15 - 1

Example – Inventory Systems

FIFO Periodic
Beg inv.	$12.00 (4 units × $3.00)
+ Purchases	37.00 (10 units × $3.70)
– End inv.	11.10 (3 units × $3.70)
= COGS	$37.90

FIFO Perpetual
Mar 14 sale	$9.00 (3 units × $3.00)
Mar 28 sale	28.90 (1 unit × $3.00) + (7 units × $3.70)
COGS	$37.90

End inv. $11.10 (3 units × $3.70)

Same Results!

© Kaplan, Inc.   16 - 1

LOS 28.c Calculate/Compare
CFAI p. 400, Schweser p. 180   Inventories

Example – Inventory Systems

Under LIFO:

Mar 1 (beg. inventory)	4 units @ $3.00 per unit
Mar 14 sale	3 units
Mar 25 purchase	10 units @ $3.70 per unit
Mar 28 sale	8 units

Periodic—last 11 units purchased are sold: one $3 unit and 10 $3.70 units

Perpetual—3 of the $3 unit are sold, 8 of the $3.70 units are sold

© Kaplan, Inc.   17 - 3

LOS 28.c Calculate/Compare
CFAI p. 400, Schweser p. 180   Inventories

Example – Inventory Systems

LIFO Periodic:

Beg inventory	$12.00 (4 units × $3.00)
+ Purchases	37.00 (10 units × $3.70)
– End inventory	9.00 (3 units × $3.00)
= COGS	$40.00

LIFO Perpetual

Mar 14 sale	$9.00 (3 units × $3.00)
Mar 28 sale	29.60 (8 units × $3.70)
COGS	$38.60
End inventory	$10.40 (1 unit × $3.00) + (2 units × $3.70)

Different Results!

© Kaplan, Inc.   18 - 1

LOS 28.c Calculate/Compare
CFAI p. 400, Schweser p. 180   Inventories

Example – Inventory Systems

Summary

Inventory System	FIFO COGS	LIFO COGS	FIFO Inventory	LIFO Inventory
Periodic	$37.90	$40.00	$11.10	$9.00
Perpetual	$37.90	$38.60	$11.10	$10.40

The inventory system only affects the LIFO and average cost flow methods.

FIFO and specific identification are unaffected.

FIFO and LIFO relationships remain!

© Kaplan, Inc.   19

LOS 28.d Compare
CFAI p. 404, Schweser p. 184   Inventories

LIFO vs. FIFO Inflationary Environment

		LIFO	FIFO
Income Statement	COGS	Higher	Lower
	EBT	Lower	Higher
	Taxes	Lower	Higher
	NI	Lower	Higher
Balance Sheet	Inv	Lower	Higher
	W/C	Lower	Higher
	R/E	Lower	Higher
Statement of Cash Flows	CFO	Higher	Lower

© Kaplan, Inc.   20

Inventories

LIFO Reserve

Firms reporting under LIFO must disclose LIFO reserve

LIFO reserve = FIFO inventory − LIFO inventory

FIFO inventory = LIFO inventory + LIFO reserve

© Kaplan, Inc.

21

Inventories

LIFO Liquidation

When a LIFO firm sells more units than it creates during a period, it is referred to as a **LIFO liquidation.**

With rising inventory costs, the effect is to reduce COGS and increase reported earnings (not sustainable).

The amount of the increase in gross income from LIFO liquidation must be disclosed.

It can be intentional (earnings manipulation) or unintentional (strikes, declining demand).

© Kaplan, Inc.

22

Inventories

Conversion from LIFO to FIFO

Balance Sheet

$\text{Inventory}_{FIFO} = \text{Inventory}_{LIFO} + \text{LIFO reserve}$

$\text{Cash}_{FIFO} \quad = \text{Cash}_{LIFO} - (\text{LIFO reserve} \times t)$

$\text{Equity}_{FIFO} \quad = \text{Equity}_{LIFO} + [\text{LIFO reserve} \times (1 - t)]$

Income Statement

$\text{COGS}_{FIFO} \quad = \text{COGS}_{LIFO} - \Delta \text{ in LIFO reserve}$

$\text{Taxes}_{FIFO} \quad = \text{Taxes}_{LIFO} + (\Delta \text{ in LIFO reserve} \times t)$

$\text{NI}_{FIFO} \quad = \text{NI}_{LIFO} + [\Delta \text{ in LIFO reserve} \times (1 - t)]$

© Kaplan, Inc.

23

Inventories

Conversion From LIFO to FIFO

20X1: LIFO inventory = 14,000   LIFO COGS = 40,000
LIFO reserve = 10,000   Net income = 2,400

20X0: LIFO reserve = 6,000

FIFO Values (@ tax rate 30%)

	Adjustment
Inventory = 14,000 + 10,000 = 24,000	+10,000
Add the reserve	
Cash = LIFO cash − 10,000 × 30%	−3,000
Higher tax with FIFO	
Equity = LIFO equity + 10,000 × (1 − 30%)	+7,000
Higher asset (inventory) value with FIFO	

© Kaplan, Inc.

24

178

Study Session 8   Financial Reporting and Analysis: Inventories, Long-Lived Assets, Income Taxes, and Non-Current Liabilities

---

Conversion From LIFO to FIFO

20X1: LIFO inventory = 14,000   LIFO COGS = 40,000
LIFO reserve = 10,000   Net income = 2,400

20X0: LIFO reserve = 6,000

FIFO Values (@ tax rate 30%)

	Adjustment
COGS = LIFO COGS – (10,000 – 6,000)	–4,000
Lower cost units in COGS	
NI = LIFO NI + (10,000 – 6,000) × (1 – 30%)	+2,800
Lower COGS increases earnings after tax	
Taxes = LIFO taxes + (10,000 – 6,000) × 30%	+1,200
Higher tax with greater gross profit	

© Kaplan, Inc.

25

Inventory Valuation (IFRS)

Lower of cost and **net realizable value**

All costs of bringing the
inventory to its current location → NRV
and condition

Excludes:

	Estimated selling X
	price
▪ Abnormal amounts	Estimated cost of (X)
▪ Storage costs	completion
▪ Admin overheads	Selling costs (X)
▪ Selling costs	NRV X

Reversal of write-downs allowed

© Kaplan, Inc.

26

Inventory Valuation (U.S. GAAP)

Lower of cost and **market value**

Same as IFRS

Current replacement cost, subject to:

Upper limit = NRV

Lower limit = (NRV – normal profit margin)

Reversal of write-downs
prohibited

© Kaplan, Inc.

27

Inventory Valuation

Under IFRS and U.S. GAAP, reporting inventory above
cost is permitted in some industries, primarily producers
and dealers of commodity-like products.

▪ Reported on the balance sheet at net realizable
value

▪ If active market exists, quoted market price is used;
otherwise, recent market transactions are used

▪ Unrealized gains/losses recognized in the income
statement

© Kaplan, Inc.

28

179

Study Session 8   Financial Reporting and Analysis: Inventories, Long-Lived Assets, Income Taxes, and Non-Current Liabilities

Slide 29

LOS 28.h Describe
CFAI p. 420, Schweser p. 193

Effects of Inventory Write-Down

Assuming write-down is added to COGS:

- COGS increase, gross and net profit margins decrease

- Inventory decreases, inventory turnover increases, days-on-hand decreases

- Current ratio decreases

- Asset turnover increases

© Kaplan, Inc.

29

Slide 30

LOS 28.i Describe
CFAI p. 425, Schweser p. 193

Inventory Disclosures

- Cost flow method used (LIFO, FIFO, etc.)

- Carrying value of inventory in total and by classification (raw materials, work-in-process, and finished goods), if appropriate

- Carrying value of inventory reported at fair value less selling costs

- COGS for the period

- Inventory write-downs for the period

- Reversals of write-downs for the period (IFRS only)

- Carrying value of pledged inventory

© Kaplan, Inc.

30

Slide 31

LOS 28.j Explain
CFAI p. 425, Schweser p. 194

Analysis of Inventory Disclosures

Condition	Possible Interpretation
Increase in raw materials and work-in-process	Expected increase in demand
Increase in finished goods alone	Decrease in demand
Finished goods growing faster than sales	Decrease in demand—may be result of excessive or obsolete inventory

© Kaplan, Inc.

31

Slide 32

LOS 28.k Calculate/Compare
CFAI p. 427, Schweser p. 195

Inventory Management Ratios

$$\text{Inventory turnover} = \frac{\text{Cost of goods sold}}{\text{Average inventory}}$$

$$\text{Days inventory on hand (DOH)} = \frac{365}{\text{Inventory turnover}}$$

$$\text{Gross profit margin} = \frac{\text{Gross profit}}{\text{Revenue}}$$

© Kaplan, Inc.

32

Study Session 8   Financial Reporting and Analysis: Inventories, Long-Lived Assets, Income Taxes, and Non-Current Liabilities

180

Profitability: LIFO vs. FIFO

LIFO is a better measure of economic cost in the <u>income statement</u> (based on more recent prices than FIFO)

With increasing prices, **LIFO** produces:

Higher COGS
Lower gross profit
Lower operating profit   Lower
Lower net profit   Margins

© Kaplan, Inc.   33

Liquidity: LIFO vs. FIFO

FIFO is a better measure of economic cost on the <u>balance sheet</u> (based on more recent prices than LIFO).

With increasing prices, **FIFO** produces:

Higher inventory balances
Higher current ratio   Higher
Higher working capital   Current Assets

© Kaplan, Inc.   34

Activity Ratios: LIFO vs. FIFO

With increasing prices, **LIFO** results in:

Higher inventory turnover
(COGS / average inventory)
Higher numerator and lower denominator

Lower days of inventory on hand
(365 / inventory turnover)
Higher denominator

© Kaplan, Inc.   35

Leverage Ratios: LIFO vs. FIFO

With increasing prices, **FIFO** results in higher inventory value than LIFO.

Both assets and equity are greater than for LIFO, resulting in lower leverage ratios.

Lower debt-to-assets ratio   Higher
Lower debt-to-equity ratio   denominators

© Kaplan, Inc.   36

181

Study Session 8   Financial Reporting and Analysis: Inventories, Long-Lived Assets, Income Taxes, and Non-Current Liabilities

---

LOS 28.I Analyze/Compare
CFAI p. 427, Schweser p. 195   Inventories

Analysis of Ratios

Condition	Possible Interpretation
Low turnover (high DOH)	Slow-moving or obsolete inventory
High turnover (low DOH) with low sales growth relative to industry	May be losing sales from insufficient inventory levels
High turnover (low DOH) with sales growth at or above industry average	Efficient inventory management

© Kaplan, Inc.   37

LOS 28.I Analyze/Compare
CFAI p. 427, Schweser p. 195   Inventories

For analytical purposes an analyst would prefer to use:

A. LIFO COGS and FIFO inventory.

B. FIFO COGS and FIFO inventory.

C. FIFO COGS and LIFO inventory.

© Kaplan, Inc.   38 - 1

Financial Reporting and Analysis

Inventories, Long-Lived Assets, Income Taxes, and Non-Current Liabilities

29. Long-Lived Assets

KAPLAN SCHOOL OF PROFESSIONAL
UNIVERSITY AND CONTINUING EDUCATION | SCHWESER

LOS 29.a Distinguish
CFAI p. 463, Schweser p. 209   Long-Lived Assets

Capitalizing vs. Expensing

Costs are **capitalized** as a balance sheet asset or **expensed** in the income statement.

Capitalizing: spreading an asset's cost over multiple periods, creating a balance sheet asset

Expensing: taking an asset's cost as an expense on the income statement in the current period

© Kaplan, Inc.   40

Study Session 8   Financial Reporting and Analysis: Inventories, Long-Lived Assets, Income Taxes, and Non-Current Liabilities

182

Capitalizing vs. Expensing

Expense if benefits beyond one period are unlikely or highly uncertain

Capitalize if benefits extend over multiple periods; amount can include additional costs to prepare the asset for use

- Subsequent expenditures that provide benefits beyond one year (replacing a roof) are capitalized.

- Subsequent expenditures that do not provide benefits beyond one year are expensed.

© Kaplan, Inc.

41

Capitalizing vs. Expensing

Interest expense on funds spent constructing a capital asset is capitalized as part of either:

- Asset's value on the balance sheet (self-use)
- Asset's value in inventory (for sale to others)

Under IFRS, capitalized interest is reduced by any income on borrowings invested temporarily.

© Kaplan, Inc.

42

Intangible Assets

Intangible assets lack physical substance.

Identifiable intangible assets:

- Can be separated from, and controlled by, the firm.

- Are expected to provide probable future benefits and their cost can be reliably measured.

Unidentifiable intangible assets cannot be separated from the firm (e.g., goodwill).

© Kaplan, Inc.

43

Purchased Intangible Assets

Purchased intangibles are recorded at cost.

For a group of assets, price paid is allocated based on fair value of each asset.

Intangibles obtained in a business acquisition

Identifiable assets recorded at fair value

Difference between purchase price and fair value of identifiable net assets reported as **goodwill**

© Kaplan, Inc.

44

Intangible Assets

Finite-lived intangibles are amortized over their useful lives (e.g., patents).

Indefinite-lived intangibles are <u>not</u> amortized but tested for impairment periodically (e.g., goodwill).

© Kaplan, Inc.   45

Internally Created Intangible Assets

Internally developed intangibles expensed as incurred except R&D, software development costs

Research costs involve discovery of new knowledge and understanding.

Development costs involve translation of research findings into a plan.

IFRS: Research costs expensed, but development costs (after technical feasibility established) may be capitalized

U.S. GAAP: Research <u>and</u> development costs expensed

© Kaplan, Inc.   46

Intangible Assets

Exception for **U.S. GAAP** is <u>software created internally</u>

Software created <u>for sale</u>

Expense costs as incurred until technical feasibility is established, then capitalize development costs

Software created <u>for internal use</u>

Expense costs as incurred until probable that project will be completed and used as intended, then capitalize development costs

© Kaplan, Inc.   47

Capitalizing vs. Expensing: Financial Statement Effects

	Capitalizing	Expensing
Assets & equity	Higher	Lower
Net income (first year)	Higher	Lower
Net income (other years)	Lower	Higher
Income variability	Lower	Higher
ROA & ROE (first year)	Higher	Lower
ROA & ROE (other years)	Lower	Higher
Debt ratio & debt-to-equity	Lower	Higher
CFO	Higher	Lower
CFI	Lower	Higher

© Kaplan, Inc.   48

Study Session 8   Financial Reporting and Analysis: Inventories, Long-Lived Assets, Income Taxes, and Non-Current Liabilities

184

Depreciation of Long-Lived Assets

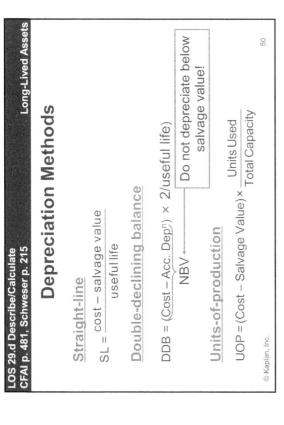

Purchase price + installation costs + transport costs → Historic cost $

Accumulated dep^n (X)

Net book value   X

B/S value, carrying value, book value

Cumulative total of depreciation expensed to I/S

Economic depreciation = decline in asset value

Analyst issue: Accounting depreciation may not equal economic depreciation.

© Kaplan, Inc.   49

Depreciation Methods

Straight-line

$$SL = \frac{cost - salvage\ value}{useful\ life}$$

Double-declining balance

$$DDB = (Cost - Acc.\ Dep^n) \times 2/useful\ life$$

NBV → Do not depreciate below salvage value!

Units-of-production

$$UOP = (Cost - Salvage\ Value) \times \frac{Units\ Used}{Total\ Capacity}$$

© Kaplan, Inc.   50

Component Depreciation

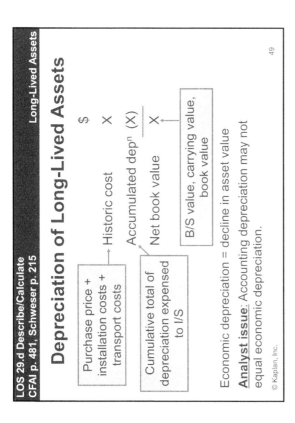

Component depreciation involves depreciating an asset based on the separate useful lives of the asset's individual components.

- Required under IFRS
- Permitted under U.S. GAAP but seldom used

Example: An office building consists of a roof, walls, elevator, HVAC, carpeting, furniture, fixtures, etc.

Issue: The firm must estimate the useful life of each component and depreciate each separately.

© Kaplan, Inc.   51

Depreciation Example

At the beginning of Year 1, a firm purchased a new machine for £4,000. The machine has an estimated life of four years or 1,000 units of production. The salvage value is estimated at £500.

Assuming the firm produces 400 units in Year 2, calculate depreciation expense for Year 2 using the following methods:

1. Straight-line
2. Double-declining balance
3. Units-of-production

© Kaplan, Inc.   52

Study Session 8 Financial Reporting and Analysis: Inventories, Long-Lived Assets, Income Taxes, and Non-Current Liabilities

185

LOS 29.d Describe/Calculate
CFAI p. 481, Schweser p. 215   **Long-Lived Assets**

Depreciation Example

Straight-line
(£4,000 cost − £500 salvage) / 4 years = £875

Double-declining balance
Year 1 = £4,000 cost × 2/4 = £2,000
Year 2 = (£4,000 cost − £2,000 Acc. Dep.) × 2/4 = £1,000

Units-of-production

$$(£4,000 \text{ cost} − £500 \text{ salvage}) \times \frac{400 \text{ units produced}}{1,000 \text{ total units}} = £1,400$$

© Kaplan, Inc.   53

LOS 29.e Describe/Calculate
CFAI p. 481, Schweser p. 218   **Long-Lived Assets**

Impact of Depreciation Method on Financial Statements

	Straight-Line	Accelerated
Depreciation expense	Lower	Higher*
Net income	Higher	Lower*
Assets	Higher	Lower
Equity	Higher	Lower
Return on assets	Higher	Lower*
Return on equity	Higher	Lower*
Turnover ratios	Lower	Higher
Cash flow	Same	Same

* **Early years** or **growing firm**

© Kaplan, Inc.   54

LOS 29.e Describe/Calculate
CFAI p. 481, Schweser p. 218   **Long-Lived Assets**

Estimates in Depreciation Calculations

Changes in salvage value and useful life both represent changes in accounting estimates

Given longer useful life or higher salvage value:

- Depreciation is lower
- EBIT, net income, and ROE are higher

Shorter lives or lower salvage values have the opposite effects.

© Kaplan, Inc.   55

Long-Lived Assets

Accelerated depreciation methods:

A. lead to higher book values than does the straight-line method.

B. result in lower net income in early years, higher net income in later years.

C. allocate larger portions of cost to later accounting periods.

© Kaplan, Inc.   56 - 1

Study Session 8   Financial Reporting and Analysis: Inventories, Long-Lived Assets, Income Taxes, and Non-Current Liabilities

186

Amortization

For intangible assets with finite lives, **amortization** spreads the asset's cost over its useful life

Estimating useful lives complicated by legal, regulatory, and economic factors

Pattern should match consumption of benefits (straight-line, accelerated, or units-of-production)

Effects of amortization choices and estimates on financial statements and ratios are the same as for depreciation

© Kaplan, Inc.

57

Revaluation Model

Alternative to the cost model under IFRS

At each revaluation date, carrying value = fair value; depreciated between revaluation dates

First revaluation date

- If fair < carrying, loss on income statement
- If fair > carrying, to equity as **revaluation surplus**

Subsequent revaluation dates

- If fair < carrying, first reduce revaluation surplus, then any remaining difference is a loss
- If fair > carrying, first reverse prior losses, then any remaining difference is revaluation surplus

© Kaplan, Inc.

58

Impairment of Long-Lived Assets

IFRS

- Annually assess indications of impairment (e.g., decline in market value or physical condition)
- Asset is impaired when carrying value > recoverable amount
- Recoverable amount is greater of "fair value less selling costs" and "value in use" (present value of future cash flows)
- If impaired, write down asset to recoverable amount and recognize loss in the income statement
- Loss reversal is <u>allowed</u> up to original impairment loss

© Kaplan, Inc.

59

Impairment of Long-Lived Assets

U.S. GAAP (2-step process)

1. Identification of impairment: Asset is impaired when book value > asset's estimated future <u>undiscounted</u> cash flows.

2. Loss recognition: If impaired, write down asset to fair value (or discounted present value of future cash flows if fair value unknown), recognize loss in income statement.

Loss reversal prohibited for assets *held-for-use*.

© Kaplan, Inc.

60

187

Study Session 8   Financial Reporting and Analysis: Inventories, Long-Lived Assets, Income Taxes, and Non-Current Liabilities

---

LOS 29.i Explain
CFAI p. 494, Schweser p. 223   Long-Lived Assets

Impairment of Long-Lived Assets

Assets Held-for-Sale (IFRS & U.S. GAAP)

- Asset is tested for impairment when transferred from *held-for-use* to *held-for-sale.*

- Depreciation expense is no longer recognized.

- Asset is impaired if book value > net realizable value (fair value – selling costs).

  - If impaired, write down asset to NRV.

  - Loss reversals are allowed up to the original loss under IFRS <u>and</u> U.S. GAAP.

© Kaplan, Inc.   61

LOS 29.i Explain
CFAI p. 494, Schweser p. 223   Long-Lived Assets

Impairment – Example

Information related to machinery owned by Milano Company follows:

	€
Original cost	500,000
Accumulated depreciation	350,000
Expected future cash flows	145,000
Fair value	140,000
Value in use	130,000
Selling costs	20,000

Assuming Milano continues to use the machinery in the future, calculate the impairment loss, if any, under both IFRS and U.S. GAAP.

© Kaplan, Inc.   62

LOS 29.i Explain
CFAI p. 494, Schweser p. 223   Long-Lived Assets

Impairment – Example

IFRS

Book value	150,000	(500,000 – 350,000)
– Recoverable amount	130,000	
Impairment loss	€20,000	

Greater of "value in use" and "fair value less selling costs"

U.S. GAAP

1. Impairment identification

   150 book value > 145 expected future cash flows

2. Loss measurement

Book value	150,000
– Fair value	140,000
Impairment loss	€10,000

© Kaplan, Inc.   63- 6

LOS 29.j Explain
CFAI p. 497, Schweser p. 225   Long-Lived Assets

Derecognition of Long-Lived Assets

	$m	
	CFI	
Proceeds	X	
Carrying value	(X)	Cost and related accumulated depreciation removed from B/S
Gain/(loss)	X/(X)	Accounting gain or loss taken to I/S

- Sales proceeds = zero for abandoned assets
- Sales proceeds = fair value if exchanged
- Discussed in MD&A and/or footnotes
- Classified as held-for-sale once sales process commences
- Held-for-sale at lower of carrying value or fair value less sales costs

© Kaplan, Inc.   64

188

Study Session 8   Financial Reporting and Analysis: Inventories, Long-Lived Assets, Income Taxes, and Non-Current Liabilities

Derecognition of Long-Lived Assets

If abandoned, sales proceeds = zero

If exchanged, sales proceeds = fair value

Discussed in MD&A and/or footnotes

Classified as held-for-sale once sales process
commences—lower of carrying value or fair value
less sales costs

65

Effects of Impairment, Revaluation, Derecognition

Impairments: Reduce asset values; reported as
expense on income statement; can be reversed
under IFRS.

Derecognition: Gain or loss reported on income
statement.

Revaluation: IFRS only; changes in fair value
can affect equity directly or be reported on the
income statement.

66

Impact of Derecognition

When asset is sold or exchanged:
- Carrying value removed from balance sheet
- Cash or new asset added to balance sheet
- Gain or loss reported on income statement

When asset is abandoned:
- Carrying value removed from balance sheet
- Any loss reported on income statement

67

Impact of Upward Asset Revaluation

Balance sheet
Increases assets (higher NBV)
Increases equity (revaluation gain)

Income statement
No impact on net income unless reversing a previous loss
Decreases future net income (increased depreciation)

68

Study Session 8   Financial Reporting and Analysis: Inventories, Long-Lived Assets, Income Taxes, and Non-Current Liabilities

189

LOS 29.k Explain/Evaluate
CFAI p. 490, Schweser p. 226   Long-Lived Assets

Impact of Upward Asset Revaluation

Cash flow

Unaffected because revaluations are non-cash gains

Disclosure

MD&A, footnotes

© Kaplan, Inc.

69

LOS 29.k Explain/Evaluate
CFAI p. 490, Schweser p. 226   Long-Lived Assets

Impact of Upward Asset Revaluation

Fixed asset and total asset turnover ratios

Decrease (higher assets)

Debt-to-equity ratio

Decreases (higher equity)

Current-year ROA and ROE

Decrease (higher assets/equity, no impact on net income unless reversing a previous loss)

Future ROA and ROE

Decrease (higher assets and equity, lower net income)

© Kaplan, Inc.

70

LOS 29.k Explain/Evaluate
CFAI p. 490, Schweser p. 226   Long-Lived Assets

Impact of Impairment

Balance sheet

Decreases assets (lower NBV)

Decreases equity (impairment charge)

Income statement

Decreases current net income (impairment charge)

Increases future net income (lower depreciation)

Impairment estimates are a potential method of earnings management.

© Kaplan, Inc.

71

LOS 29.k Explain/Evaluate
CFAI p. 490, Schweser p. 226   Long-Lived Assets

Impact of Impairment

Cash flow

Unaffected because impairments are non-cash charges

Disclosure

MD&A, footnotes

© Kaplan, Inc.

72

Study Session 8   Financial Reporting and Analysis: Inventories, Long-Lived Assets, Income Taxes, and Non-Current Liabilities

190

Impact of Impairment

Fixed asset and total asset turnover ratios
Increase (lower assets)

Debt-to-equity ratio
Increases (lower equity)

Current-year ROA and ROE
Decrease (% decrease in NI > % decrease in assets/equity)

Future ROA and ROE
Increase (lower assets/equity, higher net income)

Disclosure Requirements

Carrying value for each class of asset

Accumulated depreciation or amortization

Title restrictions and assets pledged as collateral

For impaired assets, the loss amount and circumstances

For revalued assets (IFRS only), revaluation date, how fair value determined, carrying value using historical cost model

Disclosure Requirements

Tangible Assets

Under U.S. GAAP, must disclose:

Depreciation expense for period

Balances for major classes of depreciable assets

Accumulated depreciation (in total or by major classes)

General description of depreciation methods for each major asset class

Disclosure Requirements

Tangible Assets

Under IFRS, must disclose for each class of PPE:

Measurement base, depreciation method, useful life, gross amount, and accumulated depreciation (beginning, end, and reconciliation)

Title restrictions and whether pledged as collateral

Under revaluation model, must disclose:

Date of revaluation, fair value method, carrying value under cost method, any revaluation surplus

191

Study Session 8   Financial Reporting and Analysis: Inventories, Long-Lived Assets, Income Taxes, and Non-Current Liabilities

LOS 29.l Describe
CFAI p. 499, Schweser p. 228   Long-Lived Assets

Disclosure Requirements

Intangible Assets

Under U.S. GAAP, must disclose:

1. Gross carrying amount

2. Accumulated amortization (total and by asset class)

3. Current amortization expense

4. Estimated amortization expense for next five years

© Kaplan, Inc.   77

LOS 29.l Describe
CFAI p. 499, Schweser p. 228   Long-Lived Assets

Disclosure Requirements

Intangible Assets

Under IFRS, for each class of intangible assets, must disclose whether finite or indefinite lives

If **finite**, disclosures with respect to amortization essentially the same as for depreciation

If **indefinite**, disclose carrying amount, why asset(s) have indefinite lives

© Kaplan, Inc.   78

LOS 29.l Describe
CFAI p. 499, Schweser p. 228   Long-Lived Assets

Disclosure Requirements

Impairment disclosures:

Under U.S. GAAP, description of impaired asset, why impaired, how fair value was determined, amount of loss, and where reported on financial statements

Under IFRS, for each class of assets, must disclose amount of impairments/reversals, where recognized on financials, aggregate values of main classes affected, circumstances leading to impairment/reversal

© Kaplan, Inc.   79

LOS 29.m Analyze/Interpret
CFAI p. 499, Schweser p. 229   Long-Lived Assets

Using Fixed Asset Disclosures

Analysts can use financial statement disclosures to estimate the **average age** of fixed assets and the **average depreciable life** of fixed assets.

- Identify firms with older, inefficient assets
- Identify need for major capital investments
- Identify firms with inflated earnings from the use of older assets with low depreciation

© Kaplan, Inc.   80

192

Study Session 8   Financial Reporting and Analysis: Inventories, Long-Lived Assets, Income Taxes, and Non-Current Liabilities

LOS 29.m Analyze/Interpret
CFAI p. 499, Schweser p. 229   Long-Lived Assets

Using Fixed Asset Disclosures

Estimated useful life = $\dfrac{\text{Historical cost}}{\text{Annual depreciation}}$

Estimated age = $\dfrac{\text{Accumulated depreciation}}{\text{Annual depreciation}}$

Estimated remaining life = $\dfrac{\text{Net PPE}}{\text{Annual depreciation}}$

© Kaplan, Inc.   81

LOS 29.n Compare
CFAI p. 510, Schweser p. 230   Long-Lived Assets

Investment Property (IFRS only)

Assets owned for the purpose of earning rental income and/or capital appreciation are reported as investment property.

Cost model—same as PP&E (i.e., depreciated cost), must disclose depreciation method, useful lives, fair value

Fair value model—all changes in value taken to income statement, must disclose how fair value determined

© Kaplan, Inc.   82

Long-Lived Assets

Additional LOS

LOS 29.o: effect of lease vs. purchase on financial statements

LOS 29.p how finance and operating leases affect financial statements for lessee and lessor

Leases are covered in the reading:
Non-Current (Long-Term) Liabilities

© Kaplan, Inc.   83

Financial Reporting and Analysis

Inventories, Long-Lived Assets, Income Taxes, and Non-Current Liabilities

30. Income Taxes

KAPLAN UNIVERSITY   SCHOOL OF PROFESSIONAL AND CONTINUING EDUCATION | SCHWESER

193

Study Session 8   Financial Reporting and Analysis: Inventories, Long-Lived Assets, Income Taxes, and Non-Current Liabilities

---

LOS 30.a Describe/Define
CFAI p. 550, Schweser p. 244 — Income Taxes

Income Tax Accounting

Tax Reporting

	$
Revenue	10,000
Tax allowable costs	(8,000)
Taxable income	2,000
Tax payable @ 30%	1,400

Sources of Differences

- Timing differences
- Permanent differences

Sources of Timing Differences

- Accrual vs. modified cash accounting
- Differences in reporting methods and estimates

Financial Accounting

	$
Revenue	10,000
Accrual based costs	(5,000)
Pre-tax income	5,000
Tax @ 30%	(1,500)
	3,500

$$\text{Income tax expense} = \text{Taxes payable} + \Delta\,\text{Deferred tax}$$

© Kaplan, Inc.

85

LOS 30.a Describe/Define
CFAI p. 550, Schweser p. 244 — Income Taxes

Tax Terms From the Tax Return

Taxable income: Amount of income subject to taxes

Taxes payable: Actual tax liability for the current period (based on taxable income)

Income tax paid: Actual cash flow for taxes

Tax loss carryforward: Current net taxable loss available to reduce taxes in future years; can result in deferred tax assets

Tax base: Net amount of asset or liability used for tax reporting purposes

© Kaplan, Inc.

86

LOS 30.a Describe/Define
CFAI p. 550, Schweser p. 244 — Income Taxes

Tax Terms for Financial Reporting

Accounting profit: Pre-tax financial income, earnings before tax

Income tax expense: Tax on the income statement (includes cash taxes and deferred taxes)

$$\text{Tax payable} + \Delta\,\text{DTL} - \Delta\,\text{DTA}$$

Deferred tax liability (DTL): Balance sheet item created when taxes payable < income tax expense, due to temporary differences

Deferred tax asset (DTA): Balance sheet item created when taxes payable > income tax expense, due to temporary differences

© Kaplan, Inc.

87

LOS 30.a Describe/Define
CFAI p. 550, Schweser p. 244 — Income Taxes

Tax Terms for Financial Reporting (continued)

Valuation allowance: Reserve against deferred tax assets that may not reverse in the future

Carrying value: Balance sheet value of an asset or liability

Note that both DTLs and DTAs are presented on the balance sheet, not netted

IFRS: DTL and DTA always non-current

U.S. GAAP: DTL and DTA current and non-current based on underlying asset

© Kaplan, Inc.

88

Study Session 8   Financial Reporting and Analysis: Inventories, Long-Lived Assets, Income Taxes, and Non-Current Liabilities

194

LOS 30.b Explain
CFAI p. 552, Schweser p. 245   Income Taxes

Differences: Accounting vs. Taxable Profits

- Revenues and expenses recognised in different periods for accounts and tax (e.g., warranty expenses)
- Carrying values of assets and liabilities may differ from tax values
- Tax loss carryforwards
- Specific revenues and expenses not recognized for either tax or accounting purposes

© Kaplan, Inc.

89

LOS 30.b Explain
CFAI p. 552, Schweser p. 245   Income Taxes

Deferred Tax

Deferred Tax Liability

| Tax deduction > Accounting expense |

The result is that taxable income is smaller than profit before tax and hence we pay less tax today and more tax in the future.

Deferred Tax Asset

| Tax deduction < Accounting expense |

The result is that taxable income is greater than profit before tax and hence we pay more tax today but will pay less tax in the future.

© Kaplan, Inc.

90

LOS 30.b Explain
CFAI p. 552, Schweser p. 245   Income Taxes

Deferred Tax Liabilities

Example of a deferred tax liability caused by using different depreciation methods for taxes and for financial reporting, tax rate = 40%

Tax Reporting	Yr 1
Revenue	150
Depreciation	100
Taxable income	50
Taxes payable	20

Financial Reporting	Yr 1
Revenue	150
Depreciation	50
Pre-tax income	100
Tax expense	40

© Kaplan, Inc.

91

LOS 30.b Explain
CFAI p. 552, Schweser p. 245   Income Taxes

Deferred Tax Liabilities (continued)

- Tax expense ($40 on income statement) is greater than taxes payable ($20 on tax return).
- The $20 **difference** is a deferred tax liability that is **added to the DTL** on the balance sheet.
- Under the liability method, the DTL is the tax due in the future (based on enacted tax rates) when/if the cumulative difference between taxable and pre-tax income **reverses**.

© Kaplan, Inc.

92

Slide 93

Deferred Tax Assets

Example of a deferred tax expense caused by expense for income statement greater than tax deductible expense, tax rate = 40%

	Tax Reporting	Financial Reporting	
	Yr 1		Yr 1
Revenue	150	Revenue	150
Deductible expense	50	Accrued expense	100
Taxable income	100	Pre-tax income	50
Taxes payable	40	Tax expense	20

© Kaplan, Inc.

93

Slide 94

Deferred Tax Assets (continued)

Tax expense ($20 on income statement) is less than taxes payable ($40 on tax return).

The $20 **difference** is a deferred tax asset that is **added to the DTA** on the balance sheet.

Under the liability method, the DTA is the tax avoided in the future (based on enacted tax rates) when/if the cumulative difference between taxable and pre-tax income **reverses**.

© Kaplan, Inc.

94

Slide 95

Asset Tax Base

Tax Base of Asset = amount deductible for tax purposes in future periods as economic benefits are realized

Asset purchased for $1,000

Depreciation of $200 on income statement

Carrying value = $1,000 – $200 = $800

Depreciation for tax = $400

Tax base = $1,000 – $400 = $600

Carrying value > tax base, temporary difference

Create deferred tax liability = (800 – 600) × tax rate

© Kaplan, Inc.

95

Slide 96

Liability Tax Base

A liability's tax base = carrying value minus any amounts that will be deductible for tax when the liability is settled

Liability for future warranty expense = $1,000

Carrying value = $1,000

The accrual provides no current tax deduction

Tax deductible in future as warranty expense paid

Tax base = $1,000 – $1,000 = 0

Carrying value > tax base

Timing difference, create a deferred tax asset

© Kaplan, Inc.

96

Study Session 8 Financial Reporting and Analysis: Inventories, Long-Lived Assets, Income Taxes, and Non-Current Liabilities

196

LOS 30.c Calculate
CFAI p. 555, Schweser p. 246

Income Taxes

Liability Tax Base

- Purchase materials for $1,000 on credit
- Accounts payable liability = $1,000
- Carrying value = $1,000

- This liability is tax deductible in current period, no future tax deduction when liability settled
- Tax base = $1,000 – 0 = $1,000

- Carrying value equal to tax base
- No timing difference, no deferred tax item created

© Kaplan, Inc.

97

LOS 30.d Calculate/Interpret
CFAI p. 552, Schweser p. 248

Income Taxes

Deferred Tax Liability Example

A firm acquires an asset for $21,000 with a 3-year useful life and no salvage value. The asset will generate $16,000 of annual revenue for three years. The tax rate is 30% and the firm is allowed to depreciate the asset using DDB for tax purposes but uses straight line in the accounts.

Compute the tax implications.

© Kaplan, Inc.

98

LOS 30.d Calculate/Interpret
CFAI p. 552, Schweser p. 248

Income Taxes

Deferred Tax Liability Solution

Tax Reporting

Year	1	2	3
	$	$	$
Revenue	16,000	16,000	16,000
Depreciation	(14,000)	(4,667)	(2,333)
Taxable income	2,000	11,333	13,667
Tax payable @ 30%	(600)	(3,400)	(4,100)
	1,400	7,933	9,567

© Kaplan, Inc.

99 - 4

LOS 30.d Calculate/Interpret
CFAI p. 552, Schweser p. 248

Income Taxes

Deferred Tax Liability Solution

Financial Accounts

	1	2	3
	$	$	$
Revenue	16,000	16,000	16,000
Depreciation	(7,000)	(7,000)	(7,000)
Pre-tax income	9,000	9,000	9,000
Tax expense @ 30%	(2,700)	(2,700)	(2,700)
Net income	6,300	6,300	6,300
B/S DTL	2,100	1,400	0

© Kaplan, Inc.

100 - 5

Deferred Tax Liability Solution

	1	2	3
Accounting dep^n	7,000	7,000	7,000
Tax return dep^n	(14,000)	(4,667)	(2,333)
Difference	(7,000)	2,333	4,667
Tax rate	30%	30%	30%
Δ DTL	(2,100)	700	1,400
Tax payable	(600)	(3,400)	(4,100)
Δ DTL	(2,100)	700	1,400
Tax expense	(2,700)	(2,700)	(2,700)

© Kaplan, Inc.   101-6

Deferred Tax Asset Example

A firm has revenues of $8,000 for each of three years. The firm estimates the warranty expense to be 12.5% of revenues each year. The actual expenditure of $3,000 to meet warranty claims was not made until the third year. The tax rate is 30%.

Tax Reporting

	1	2	3
	$	$	$
Revenue	8,000	8,000	8,000
Repairs	-	-	(3,000)
Taxable income	8,000	8,000	5,000
Tax payable @ 30%	(2,400)	(2,400)	(1,500)
	5,600	5,600	3,500

© Kaplan, Inc.   102-2

Deferred Tax Asset Solution

Financial Accounts

	1	2	3
	$	$	$
Revenue	8,000	8,000	8,000
Warranty expense	(1,000)	(1,000)	(1,000)
Pre-tax income	7,000	7,000	7,000
Tax expense@ 30%	(2,100)	(2,100)	(2,100)
PAT	4,900	4,900	4,900
B/S DTA	300	600	0

© Kaplan, Inc.   103-5

Deferred Tax Asset Solution

	1	2	3
Accounting expense	1,000	1,000	1,000
Tax return expense	0	0	(3,000)
Difference	1,000	1,000	(2,000)
Tax rate	30%	30%	30%
Δ DTA	300	300	(600)
Tax payable	(2,400)	(2,400)	(1,500)
Δ DTA	300	300	(600)
Tax expense	(2,100)	(2,100)	(2,100)

© Kaplan, Inc.   104

Study Session 8   Financial Reporting and Analysis: Inventories, Long-Lived Assets, Income Taxes, and Non-Current Liabilities

198

A deferred tax asset would *most likely* be created by:

A. using straight-line depreciation for financial reporting and using an accelerated method for tax returns.

B. differing treatment of warranty expenses for taxes and for financial reporting.

C. utilizing an existing tax loss carryforward to reduce a given year's taxes payable.

© Kaplan, Inc.

105 - 1

LOS 30.d Calculate/Interpret
CFAI p. 552; Schweser p. 248

Liability Method for Deferred Taxes

DTAs and DTLs are based on differences that are **expected to reverse.**

DTA and DTL values are adjusted for changes in future **tax rates** for the period(s) when differences are expected to reverse.

© Kaplan, Inc.

106

LOS 30.e Evaluate
CFAI p. 559; Schweser p. 252

Effect of a Change in Tax Rate

When the **tax rate** *decreases:*
Deferred tax liability ↓   Income tax expense ↓
Deferred tax asset   ↓   Income tax expense ↑

When the **tax rate** *increases:*
Deferred tax liability ↑   Income tax expense ↑
Deferred tax asset   ↑   Income tax expense ↓

tax expense = tax payable + ΔDTL − ΔDTA

Net effect depends on relative sizes of DTL and DTA.

© Kaplan, Inc.

107

LOS 30.e Evaluate
CFAI p. 559; Schweser p. 252

Tax Rate Change Example

At the end of the year, a firm with a tax rate of 30% reports a DTL of $30 million and DTA of $20 million. At the beginning of the next year, the tax rate is increased to 35%.
What is the effect of the tax rate change on the existing DTL and existing DTA?

New DTL = 35/30 × $30 = $35 million (+ $5 million)

New DTA = 35/30 × $20 = $23.3 million (+ $3.3 million)

© Kaplan, Inc.

108

199

Study Session 8   Financial Reporting and Analysis: Inventories, Long-Lived Assets, Income Taxes, and Non-Current Liabilities

Tax Rate Change Example

New DTL = 35/30 × $30 = $35 million (+ $5 million)

New DTA = 35/30 × $20 = $23.3 million (+ $3.33 million)

What is the effect of these changes on reported net income at the end of the year?

Income tax expense = tax payable + Δ DTL – Δ DTA

Net increase in income tax expense = 5 – 3.33 = 1.67 mill

Tax expense up $1.67 million, net income down, equity decreased

© Kaplan, Inc.   109

DTL with Tax Rate Change

Asset cost = 24,000, 3-year life, SL depreciation for financials, DDB depreciation for tax, tax rate is 40%, changes to 35% at the end of Year 2. Calculate DTL at the end of each year.

Year	1	2	3
Tax depreciation	16,000	5,333	2,667
Tax base	8,000	2,667	0
Financial depreciation	8,000	8,000	8,000
Carrying value	16,000	8,000	0

© Kaplan, Inc.   110

DTL with Tax Rate Change

Year end	1	2	3
Carrying value	16,000	8,000	0
Tax base	–8,000	–2,667	0
Difference	8,000	5,333	0
Tax Rate	× 40%	× 35%	× 35%
DTL	3,200	1,867	0

At a point in time, DTL = (CV – tax base) × future tax rate

© Kaplan, Inc.   111

Effects of Tax Rate Change

Effect on taxes payable:

A **decrease in future tax rates** will decrease taxes payable and (other things equal) increase future net income and operating cash flow.

An **increase in future tax rates** will increase taxes payable and (other things equal) decrease future net income and operating cash flow.

© Kaplan, Inc.   112

200

Study Session 8   Financial Reporting and Analysis: Inventories, Long-Lived Assets, Income Taxes, and Non-Current Liabilities

Permanent Differences

Differences between tax and financial reporting that *will not* reverse in the future do not cause deferred tax

- Tax exempt income or non-deductible expenses
- Tax credits for some expenditures

Result: effective tax rate ≠ statutory rate

$$\frac{\text{Income tax expense}}{\text{Pretax income}}$$

© Kaplan, Inc.   113

Business Combinations

No deferred tax on goodwill or goodwill impairments

Deferred tax may arise from adjustment of carrying values of acquired assets and liabilities to fair value.

Subsidiaries, JVs, Associates

Recognition of earnings vs. dividends

Deferred tax (DTL) unless:

- Parent controls timing of reversal
  - Timing difference is unlikely to reverse

© Kaplan, Inc.   114

Valuation Allowance

A valuation allowance reduces a deferred tax asset

Based on the likelihood that the asset will not be realized (e.g., no taxable income expected)

U.S. GAAP – Full DTA shown, offset by valuation allowance

IFRS – DTA shown is adjusted for probability that the asset will be not be realized

© Kaplan, Inc.   115

Valuation Allowance

Valuation allowance can be used to manipulate income:

- Increasing the allowance will decrease income
- Decreasing the allowance will increase income

May affect analysts' assumptions regarding future earnings prospects and cash flows

© Kaplan, Inc.   116

LOS 30.h Explain
CFAI p. 566, Schweser p. 256   Income Taxes

Recognition and Measurement

Current and deferred taxes recognized on the income statement unless they are taken directly to equity

Carrying amounts of deferred tax items affected by changes in tax rates or recoverability estimates

Taxes and deferred taxes taken directly to equity for:

PP&E revaluations (IFRS); long-term investments under fair value method; changes in accounting policies; adjustments to DTL because estimated recovery is reduced.

© Kaplan, Inc.   117

LOS 30.i Analyze/Explain
CFAI p. 570, Schweser p. 257   Income Taxes

Comparison of Deferred Tax Items

Analyst should examine disclosures showing:

Change in DTLs by source/category
(e.g., excess of tax over book depreciation)

Change in DTAs by source/category
(e.g., write-down of inventory)

Change in valuation allowance

© Kaplan, Inc.   118

LOS 30.i Analyze/Explain
CFAI p. 570, Schweser p. 257   Income Taxes

Required Deferred Tax Disclosures

Deferred tax liabilities/assets, any valuation allowance, and net change in valuation allowance

Unrecognized deferred tax liability for **undistributed earnings of subsidiaries** and joint ventures

Current-year tax effect of each type of temporary difference

© Kaplan, Inc.   119

LOS 30.i Analyze/Explain
CFAI p. 570, Schweser p. 257   Income Taxes

Required Deferred Tax Disclosures

Components of income tax expense

Tax loss **carryforwards and credits**

Reconciliation of difference between tax expense as a % of pre-tax income and statutory tax rate

© Kaplan, Inc.   120

Study Session 8   Financial Reporting and Analysis: Inventories, Long-Lived Assets, Income Taxes, and Non-Current Liabilities

202

Key Differences—IFRS, U.S. GAAP

IFRS only: Revaluation model – deferred tax to equity

Undistributed profits from subsidiaries:

IFRS: No DTL if investor firm can control distribution and probable that will not reverse

U.S. GAAP: DTL recognized on temporary differences

Deferred tax assets:

IFRS: Recognized if recovery probable

U.S. GAAP: Full recognition, reduced by valuation allowance

Presentation:

U.S. GAAP: Current and non-current

IFRS: All non-current

© Kaplan, Inc.   122

Bond Terminology

Par value   ⟶ The face value to be paid at maturity

Coupon rate   ⟶ Stated rate used to calculate the coupon payment

Initial liability ⟶ Issue price (PV of future cash flows discounted at the market rate of interest at issuance)

**Effective   ⟶ The discount rate (IRR, YTM) that equates
Interest Rate**   PV of future cash flows (coupon payments and par value) with the issue price

**Interest
Expense**   ⟶ Book value × Effective interest rate

© Kaplan, Inc.   124

Analysis of Deferred Tax Disclosures

Be aware of **differences** in tax reconciliation between **periods**

Look for cumulative differences due to **asset impairments and post-retirement benefits**

Restructuring charges can create a deferred tax asset (not currently tax deductible)

© Kaplan, Inc.   121

Inventories, Long-Lived Assets, Income Taxes, and Non-Current (Long-Term) Liabilities

31. Non-Current (Long-Term) Liabilities

KAPLAN UNIVERSITY   SCHOOL OF PROFESSIONAL AND CONTINUING EDUCATION   **SCHWESER**

Financial Statement Effects of Debt Issuance

On **balance sheet**, create a liability equal to proceeds received

On **income statement**, interest expense = beginning of period book value × market rate at issuance

On **cash flow statement**

- CFO is reduced by cash (coupon) interest
- CFF is increased by proceeds at issuance
- CFF is decreased by principal paid at maturity

© Kaplan, Inc.   125

Bonds Issued at Face Value
Market rate = Coupon rate

Balance sheet

- Initial liability is equal to issue price, which is face value.
- Liability remains at face value over bond term (no amortization required).
- Face amount is repaid at maturity.

Income statement

- Interest expense = Book value × Market rate at issuance
- Since market rate and coupon rate are the same, expense is equal to the coupon payment.

© Kaplan, Inc.   126

Bonds Issued at a Discount
Market rate > Coupon rate

Balance sheet

- Initial liability equal to issue price, which is *less* than face
- Liability *increases* over time as the discount is amortized
- Book value is equal to PV of remaining cash flows discounted at the market rate at issuance
- Face amount (including discount) is repaid at maturity

Income statement

- Interest expense = Book value × market rate at issuance
- Expense *increases* over time as BV increases to face

© Kaplan, Inc.   127

Bonds Issued at a Premium
Coupon rate > Market rate

Balance sheet

- Initial liability equal to issue price, which is *higher* than face
- Liability *decreases* over time as the premium is amortized
- Book value is equal to PV of remaining cash flows discounted at the market rate at issuance
- Face amount is repaid at maturity (borrower keeps premium)

Income statement

- Interest expense = book value × market rate at issuance
- Expense *decreases* over time as BV declines to face

© Kaplan, Inc.   128

204

Study Session 8   Financial Reporting and Analysis: Inventories, Long-Lived Assets, Income Taxes, and Non-Current Liabilities

---

Amortization of Premium/Discount

Effective Interest Method of Amortization

- Interest expense is equal to YTM at issuance times beginning balance sheet liability.

- Difference between coupon interest and interest expense is amortization of premium of discount.

  - Required under IFRS, preferred under U.S. GAAP

Straight-line Amortization of Premium/Discount

- Annual amortization is discount/years or premium/years

- Interest expense is coupon +/– amortization

  - Permitted under U.S. GAAP

© Kaplan, Inc.

129

Accounting for Premium Bonds

Illiquid Corporation issues a 3-year, $1,000 par value bond with an annual coupon of 20% at $1,130.88. The market interest rate is 14.33%. Using the effective interest method:

	Balance Sheet Liability	Interest Expense	Coupon Int. Paid	Premium Amortization
Year 1	1,130.88	162.06	200	–37.94
Year 2	1,092.94	156.62	200	–43.38
Year 3	1,049.56	150.40	200	–49.60
Bond redemption	1,000			

© Kaplan, Inc.

130

Accounting for Premium Bonds

Illiquid Corporation issues a 3-year, $1,000 par value bond with an annual coupon of 20% at $1,130.88. The market interest rate is 14.33%. Using straight-line amortization:

	Balance Sheet Liability	Interest Expense	Coupon Int. Paid	Premium Amortization
Year 1	1,130.88	156.37	200	–43.63
Year 2	1,087.25	156.37	200	–43.63
Year 3	1,043.62	156.38	200	–43.62
Bond redemption	1,000			

© Kaplan, Inc.

131

Issuance Costs

Costs incurred at time of issuance for legal fees, commissions, printing, etc.

IFRS

- Deducted from initial bond liability
- Result is higher effective interest rate

U.S. GAAP

- Shown on balance sheet as a prepaid expense (deferred charge)
  - Controversial treatment because asset does not provide future economic benefits
- Amortized over the bond's life

© Kaplan, Inc.

132

205

Study Session 8 Financial Reporting and Analysis: Inventories, Long-Lived Assets, Income Taxes, and Non-Current Liabilities

Effect of Changing Interest Rates

- Inverse relationship between the **market value** (fair value) of debt and interest rates

- Once debt is issued, firms report the book value (not market value) of debt; **changes in interest rates do not affect balance sheet or income statement.**

  Δ interest rate: carrying value ≠ fair value

- Exception: liabilities hedged with derivatives "fair value hedges"

© Kaplan, Inc.

134

Debt Extinguishment

B/S carrying value	$
Repurchase price	X
Gain/(Loss)	(X)
Unamortized issuance costs	X/(X)
Gain/(Loss) on repurchase	(X)
	X/(X)

U.S. GAAP only

- I/S continuing operations
- No gain/loss at maturity
- Gain or loss if repurchased prior to maturity

Repurchase > carrying value = loss

Repurchase < carrying value = gain

Detail in MD&A, footnotes

© Kaplan, Inc.

136

Acme issues an 8%, 10-year annual-pay bond when market yield is 7.5% for $1,034.32.

Impact of the bond on net income in the first year is:

A. –$80.00, and NI is less than with equal proceeds from par debt.

B. –$77.57, and NI is more than with equal proceeds from par debt.

C. –$77.57, and NI is the same as with equal proceeds from par debt.

© Kaplan, Inc.

133 - 2

Effect of Changing Interest Rates

For analysis, market value is more relevant than book value.

- Market value reflects the cost to buy back the debt and cancel the liability.

- Lower market values reflect stronger solvency positions.

IFRS and U.S. GAAP give firms irrevocable option to report debt at fair value.

© Kaplan, Inc.

135

206

Study Session 8   Financial Reporting and Analysis: Inventories, Long-Lived Assets, Income Taxes, and Non-Current Liabilities

Covenants

Restrictions placed on borrower to protect lender

Violation = technical default (lender can demand payment)

Affirmative covenants – borrower agrees to:

- Make timely payment of principal and interest
- Maintain certain ratios (current ratio, D/E, coverage, etc.)
- Maintain collateral and pay taxes

Negative covenants – borrower will refrain from:

- Paying dividends and repurchasing shares
- Engaging in mergers and acquisitions
- Issuing more debt

© Kaplan, Inc.   137

Disclosure of Long-Term Debt

B/S split between:

- Current liabilities
- Long-term liabilities

Footnotes

- Nature of the liabilities
- Maturity dates
- Stated and effective interest rates
- Call provisions and conversion privileges
- Restrictions imposed by creditors
- Assets pledged as security
- Amount of debt maturing in each of the next five years

© Kaplan, Inc.   138

Reasons to Lease

Alternative to borrowing and purchasing asset

Advantages:

1. Short period of use
2. Cheaper financing (potentially)
3. No down payment
4. Fixed rates
5. May have fewer covenants
6. Less risk of obsolescence
7. Potential financial reporting adv (op lease)
8. Tax advantages—synthetic leases

© Kaplan, Inc.   139

Finance (Capital) vs. Operating Lease

U.S. GAAP: Treat **as capital lease** if any of the following criteria are met:

1. Title to the leased asset is transferred to the lessee at the end of the lease.
2. A bargain purchase option exists.
3. The lease period is at least 75% of the asset's economic life.
4. The PV of the lease payments ≥ 90% of the leased asset's fair value.

IFRS: Treat as **finance lease** if substantially all rights and risks of ownership are transferred (no quantitative criteria).

© Kaplan, Inc.   140

Non-Current (Long-Term)
Liabilities

Treatment of Finance Lease

Treat **as if leased asset were purchased** with debt.

- Lower of fair value or PV of future lease payments is reported as a **balance sheet asset and liability.**

  - Asset is **depreciated** over time.

  - Interest expense on liability is recognized.

  - Lease payments treated like amortizing debt — each payment is **part interest and part principal.**

© Kaplan, Inc.

141

Non-Current (Long-Term)
Liabilities

Finance Lease Example

Firm leases asset for three years

Payments = $10,000 year

Straight-line depreciation, no salvage value

Fair market value = $27,000

Lease discount rate = 7%

Use lower of:

$26,243

Balance Sheet Effects:

Asset = PV lease payments   I/Y = 7

Liability = PV lease payments   N = 3

PMT = $10,000

© Kaplan, Inc.

142

Non-Current (Long-Term)
Liabilities

Finance Lease Example (continued)

Year	Beg. value	Interest expense @7%	Payment	Year-end lease value	Book value asset
1	26,243	1,837	10,000	18,080	17,495
2	18,080	1,266	10,000	9,346	8,747
3	9,346	654	10,000	0	0

Principal payment = $10,000 − interest

Depreciation = $26,243 ÷ 3 = $8,748/year

$18,080 long-term, $8,163 current, total $26,243

© Kaplan, Inc.

143

Non-Current (Long-Term)
Liabilities

Finance Lease Example (continued)

	CFO (Interest)	CFF (Principal)
1	1,837	10,000 − 1,837 = 8,163
2	1,266	10,000 − 1,266 = 8,734
3	654	10,000 − 654 = 9,346

Operating lease CFO = $10,000 annual outflow

Rent expense = $10,000/year

Finance lease expense = interest + depreciation

Net income in early years lower for finance lease

CFO higher, CFF lower for finance lease

© Kaplan, Inc.

144

208

Study Session 8   Financial Reporting and Analysis: Inventories, Long-Lived Assets, Income Taxes, and Non-Current Liabilities

Finance vs. Operating Lease

Financial Statement Totals	Finance	Operating
Assets	Higher	Lower
Liabilities	Higher	Lower
Net income (early years)	Lower	Higher
Net income (later years)	Higher	Lower
Total Net Income	Same	Same
Cash flow from operations	Higher	Lower
Cash flow from financing	Lower	Higher
Total cash flow	Same	Same

© Kaplan, Inc.

146

Lessor Reporting with Finance Lease

Lessor reports **lease receivable** on balance sheet equal to PV of minimum lease payments and estimated residual value of asset

Leased asset is derecognized (removed from balance sheet)

Lease payments are part interest, part return of capital

© Kaplan, Inc.

148

Income Statement Effects

	Finance (Capital) Lease			Operating Lease
Year	Interest	Dep^n	Total	Rental Expense
1	$1,837	$8,748	$10,585	$10,000
2	$1,266	$8,748	$10,014	$10,000
3	$654	$8,747	$9,401	$10,000
Total	$3,757	$26,243	$30,000	$30,000

Early years: higher expenses → lower NI with finance lease
Later years: lower expenses → higher NI with finance lease

© Kaplan, Inc.

145 - 2

If Acme reports its lease of equipment as an operating lease rather than as a capital lease, the effect in the first year would be to:

A. increase net income and decrease CFO.

B. increase net income and CFO.

C. decrease net income and increase CFO.

© Kaplan, Inc.

147 - 1

Slide 149

Lessor Reporting with Finance Lease

Under IFRS

If lessor is **manufacturer or dealer:**

- Sales revenue is lower of asset fair value or PV of minimum lease payments

- Initial direct costs of lease treated as expense

- Cost of sale is carrying value of asset minus PV of estimated residual value

- Profit typically recorded at time of sale

© Kaplan, Inc.

149

Slide 150

Lessor Reporting with Finance Lease

Under U.S. GAAP

If lease receivable = carrying value,

direct financing lease, interest income over the lease term

If lease receivable > carrying value,

sales-type lease, income from **gross profit at inception of lease** plus interest income over the lease term

© Kaplan, Inc.

150

Slide 151

Direct Financing Lease – Example

Rowlands, Inc., leases a machine to Hall Company. The lease qualifies as a finance lease. The terms of the lease are three years at $10,000 p.a. Rowlands estimates that the machine can be sold in three years for $5,000. The asset cost $24,000.

Rate Implicit in the Lease {
N   3
PMT $10,000   CPT I/Y = 19.897%
FV $5,000
PV   ($24,000)
}

© Kaplan, Inc.

151

Slide 152

Direct Financing Lease – Example

Year	Beginning lease receivable	Interest income	Annual end-of-year lease payment	Reduction in lease receivable	Year-end lease receivable
1	24,000	4,775	10,000	5,225	18,775
2	18,775	3,736	10,000	6,264	12,511
3	12,511	2,489	10,000	7,511	5,000
Total		11,000	30,000	19,000	

CFO

CFI permitted IFRS

CFI

CFO if leasing company

© Kaplan, Inc.

152

Study Session 8   Financial Reporting and Analysis: Inventories, Long-Lived Assets, Income Taxes, and Non-Current Liabilities

210

Non-Current (Long-Term)
Liabilities

Lease Disclosure

Lessees and lessors are required to disclose:

General description of leasing arrangements

Separately for operating and finance leases:

Undiscounted amount of lease payments to be paid

➢ In each of the next five years

➢ Aggregated payments beyond five years

Lease revenue and expense for each period presented in the income statement

For finance leases (in addition to above):

PV of lease payments and interest portion by year

© Kaplan, Inc.

153

Non-Current (Long-Term)
Liabilities

Under IFRS a lessor would be *most likely* to recognize depreciation expense related to a leased asset for a lease classified as a(n):

A. operating lease.

B. financing lease.

C. sales-type lease.

© Kaplan, Inc.

154 - 2

Non-Current (Long-Term)
Liabilities

Defined Contribution Plan Reporting

Income Statement

Pension expense = employer's contribution

Balance Sheet

▪ No future obligation to report as a liability

▪ Decrease in cash, or increase in current liability if not paid by fiscal year-end

© Kaplan, Inc.

155

Non-Current (Long-Term)
Liabilities

Defined Benefit Plan Reporting

Balance Sheet

Plan assets < estimated obligation: Net liability

Plan assets > estimated obligation: Net asset

Must estimate PV of pension obligations using:

Future compensation levels   Employee turnover

Average retirement age   Mortality rates

Appropriate discount rate

© Kaplan, Inc.

156

211

Study Session 8   Financial Reporting and Analysis: Inventories, Long-Lived Assets, Income Taxes, and Non-Current Liabilities

Defined Benefit Plan Reporting

<u>Change</u> in net pension asset or liability during year

- **Service costs**: PV of additional benefits earned
- **Past service costs**: Retroactive benefits awarded when plan is initiated or changed
- **Net interest expense/income**: Beginning value × assumed discount rate
- **Actuarial gains/losses**: Changes in assumptions
- **Return on plan assets**

Pension expense or other comprehensive income?
Different treatments under IFRS and U.S. GAAP

© Kaplan, Inc.   157

Defined Benefit Plan Reporting

Change in net pension asset/liability during period

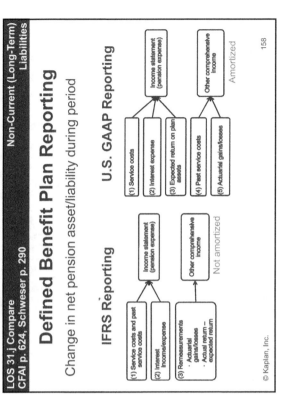

IFRS Reporting   **U.S. GAAP Reporting**

© Kaplan, Inc.   158

Defined Benefit Plan Reporting

Manufacturing companies allocate pension expense

- **Inventory** or **cost of goods sold** for employees who provide direct labor to production
- **Salary and administrative expense** for other employees

Pension expense details are disclosed in the financial statement notes

© Kaplan, Inc.   159

Solvency

Solvency measures the firm's ability to satisfy its long-term obligations.

Leverage ratios
  Balance sheet focus of measuring the amount of debt in the firm's capital structure

Coverage ratios
  Income statement focus of measuring the sufficiency of earnings to repay interest and other fixed charges

© Kaplan, Inc.   160

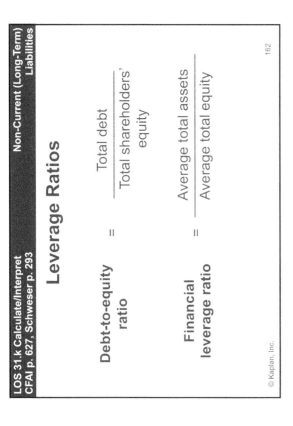

1) If a firm chooses to expense the purchase price of an asset, rather than capitalize it, the effects on CFO and ROA are *most likely* to be:

CFO	**ROA**
A. Unchanged	Lower
B. Lower	Lower
C. Unchanged	Unchanged

© Kaplan, Inc.

- 3

2) Filer, Inc., has a deferred tax asset of $30 million and a deferred tax liability of $40 million at year-end 20X1 based on their tax rate of 35%. If Filer's future tax rate will be 40% rather than 35%, the effect of the change on Filer's 20X1 year-end equity would be a(n):

A. increase of $1.25 million.

B. decrease of $1.43 million.

C. decrease of $1.25 million.

© Kaplan, Inc.

- 4

3) If a firm chooses to report a lease as an operating lease rather than as a finance lease, the *most likely* effect in the first year of the lease is a decrease in the firm's:

A. current ratio.

B. net income.

C. operating earnings.

© Kaplan, Inc.

- 2

4) A company issues a 10-year 7% annual-pay bond and receives proceeds of $900 per $1,000 face value. Under the effective interest rate method, the interest expense that will be reported per $1,000 face value for the second year after issuance is *closest* to:

A. $70.00.

B. $76.77.

C. $77.34.

© Kaplan, Inc.

- 2

Study Session 8   Financial Reporting and Analysis: Inventories, Long-Lived Assets, Income Taxes, and Non-Current Liabilities

214

Additional Problems

5) The following information is for Perla Corp.:

Inventory at cost = 8.45 million

Completion costs = 1.4 million

Expected sales price = 9.55 million

Selling expenses = 4%

Normal profit margin = 12%

If Perla reports under IFRS, its inventory value is:

A. 7.77 million.

B. 8.45 million.

C. 9.17 million.

© Kaplan, Inc.

-2

STUDY SESSION 8 ANSWERS

Reading	Slide Number	Answer
28	38	A
29	56	B
30	105	B
31	133	C
31	147	A
31	154	A

Additional Problems

1. B

2. B

3. C

4. C

5. A

Study Session 9

Financial Reporting and Analysis: Financial Reporting Quality and Financial Statement Analysis

Financial Reporting Quality and Financial Statement Analysis

32. Financial Reporting Quality

Study Session 9
Financial Reporting Quality and Financial Statement Analysis

32. Financial Reporting Quality
33. Financial Statement Analysis: Applications

LOS 32.b Describe
CFAI p. 644, Schweser p. 305

Financial Reports Quality Spectrum

High quality

Adheres to GAAP, decision-useful,
  earnings adequate, sustainable

Adheres to GAAP, decision-useful,
  but earnings low or not sustainable

Compliant with GAAP but biased choices

Compliant with GAAP but earnings managed

Not compliant with GAAP, but reflects firm's actual activity

Not compliant with GAAP, fictitious or fraudulent numbers

Low quality

3 - 5

LOS 32.a Distinguish
CFAI p. 643, Schweser p. 304

Financial Statements

Financial reporting quality is high if:

- Reporting is compliant with GAAP
- Information is relevant, neutral, complete, free from errors, and decision-useful
- Statements faithfully represent economic reality of activities and financial position

Earnings quality is high if:

- Earnings are sustainable
- Earnings provide adequate return to investors

2

Biased Accounting Choices

Financial reports are most decision-useful when they are **unbiased** (neutral).

Aggressive accounting choices increase current period earnings and financial position.
Conservative accounting choices decrease current period earnings and financial position.

Conservative bias can also result from accounting standards themselves (e.g., accounting for R&D and accounting for oil and gas exploration).

© Kaplan, Inc.

4

Biased Accounting Choices

Management may **smooth earnings** by making conservative choices when earnings are high and aggressive choices when earnings are low.

Management can introduce bias by presenting reports that emphasize good news and/or obscure bad news.

© Kaplan, Inc.

5

Conditions for Low-Quality Reporting

1. Motivations
   - To meet or exceed benchmark EPS (e.g., prior year EPS, analyst expectations)
   - To increase compensation and reputation
   - To increase stock price
   - To avoid violating debt covenants (highly leveraged, unprofitable companies)
   - To improve view of company by investors, suppliers, customers

© Kaplan, Inc.

6

Conditions for Low-Quality Reporting

2. Opportunity
   - Weak internal controls
   - Inadequate board oversight
   - Range of acceptable treatments within GAAP
   - Minimal consequences for inappropriate choices

3. Rationalization
   Managers create reasons to justify their behavior

© Kaplan, Inc.

7

LOS 32.f Describe
CFAI p. 660, Schweser p. 309   **Financial Reporting Quality**

Mechanisms that Discipline Financial Reporting Quality

1. Government regulation
   - Securities registration
   - Disclosure requirements
   - Auditing requirements
   - Management commentary, review of business, principal risks and uncertainties
   - Management responsibility for reporting
   - Review of filings
   - Enforcement: fines, suspension, prosecution

© Kaplan, Inc.

8

LOS 32.f Describe
CFAI p. 660, Schweser p. 309   **Financial Reporting Quality**

Mechanisms that Discipline Financial Reporting Quality

2. **Auditors** provide opinion on financial reporting:
   - In U.S., auditor must assess internal controls
   - Does not guarantee absence of errors/fraud
   - Auditor is selected, paid by company

3. **Private contracts** may have loan covenants, specific methods to calculate accounting measures, and financial triggers for return of investment.

© Kaplan, Inc.

9

LOS 32.g Describe
CFAI p. 667, Schweser p. 310   **Financial Reporting Quality**

Non-GAAP Presentation

Companies may present non-GAAP (pro forma) accounting measures designed to influence analysts' earnings expectations and valuations.

Non-GAAP measures often remove negative items.

SEC: Non-GAAP measure cannot be more prominent; must disclose GAAP measure and reconcile.

IFRS: Non-GAAP measures defined, explanation for their use, reconciliation with closest GAAP measure

© Kaplan, Inc.

10

LOS 32.h Describe
CFAI p. 672, Schweser p. 310   **Financial Reporting Quality**

Accounting Choices and Estimates

Revenue recognition choices

- Shipping terms: Recognize at shipping point or destination
- Discounts to increase orders in current period
- Delay shipments to defer revenue to later period
- Increase shipments to distributors ("channel stuffing")
- Bill-and-hold transactions: Recognize revenue for goods that have not been shipped

© Kaplan, Inc.

11

LOS 32.h Describe
CFAI p. 672, Schweser p. 310   **Financial Reporting Quality**

Accounting Choices and Estimates

Management of accruals
Allowance for bad debt, warranty expense

Depreciation method
Straight-line versus accelerated

Depreciation estimates
Economic life, salvage value

© Kaplan, Inc.   12

LOS 32.h Describe
CFAI p. 672, Schweser p. 310   **Financial Reporting Quality**

Accounting Choices and Estimates

Valuation allowance
Contra account to deferred tax asset

Inventory cost flow assumptions
With increasing prices, FIFO COGS are less than
AVCO COGS, which are less than LIFO COGS

Capitalization versus expensing
Capitalization defers expenses to future periods

© Kaplan, Inc.   13

LOS 32.h Describe
CFAI p. 672, Schweser p. 310   **Financial Reporting Quality**

Accounting Choices and Estimates

Impairments
Delaying recognition of impairment charges

Related-party transactions
Can move earnings into or out of the firm

© Kaplan, Inc.   14

LOS 32.h Describe
CFAI p. 672, Schweser p. 310   **Financial Reporting Quality**

Accounting Choices and Estimates

Managing operating cash flow
- Capitalizing purchases
- Stretching payables
- Capitalizing cash interest/expensing amortized
  discount

Under IFRS:
- Classifying interest and dividends paid as CFF
  (rather than CFO)
- Classifying dividends and interest received as CFO
  (rather than CFI)

© Kaplan, Inc.   15

LOS 32.i Describe
CFAI p. 689, Schweser p. 314   **Financial Reporting Quality**

Accounting Warning Signs

Warning signs indicate more analysis is required; determine if there is a business purpose or if financial statements are being manipulated

Multiple warning signs without an adequate explanation: consider avoiding the investment

© Kaplan, Inc.   16

LOS 32.i Describe
CFAI p. 689, Schweser p. 314   **Financial Reporting Quality**

Accounting Warning Signs

Revenue recognition warning signs:

- Revenue growth out of line with peers
- Change in revenue recognition method
- Bill-and-hold transactions
- Changes in rebate estimates
- Receivables turnover, total asset turnover decreasing over time
- Non-operating or one-time items included in revenue

© Kaplan, Inc.   17

LOS 32.i Describe
CFAI p. 689, Schweser p. 314   **Financial Reporting Quality**

Accounting Warning Signs

Inventory warning signs:

- Inventory turnover ratio declining over time
- Decrease in inventory under LIFO: results in unsustainably low COGS (high earnings)

Capitalization and **cash flow** warning signs:

- Capitalization of costs that industry peers do not capitalize
- Ratio of CFO to net income is consistently less than one or declining over time

© Kaplan, Inc.   18

LOS 32.i Describe
CFAI p. 689, Schweser p. 314   **Financial Reporting Quality**

Accounting Warning Signs

Other warning signs:

- Depreciation methods, useful lives, salvage values out of line with peers
- Fourth quarter earnings surprises
- Significant related-party transactions
- Recurring "non-recurring expenses"
- Lack of transparency and disclosure
- Emphasis on non-GAAP earnings measures
- Numerous acquisitions

© Kaplan, Inc.   19

Financial Reporting and Analysis

Financial Reporting Quality and Financial Statement Analysis

33. Financial Statement Analysis: Applications

KAPLAN UNIVERSITY   SCHOOL OF PROFESSIONAL AND CONTINUING EDUCATION | SCHWESER

LOS 33.a Evaluate/Explain
CFAI p. 705, Schweser p. 321

Financial Statement Analysis: Applications

Evaluating Past Financial Performance

- How have key ratios changed and why?
- How do key ratios and trends compare with competitors/industry?
- Which aspects of performance are critical for a competitive advantage?
- How did the company perform in these areas?
- What is the company's business model and strategy—are they reflected in key measures?

© Kaplan, Inc.   21

LOS 33.b Forecast
CFAI p. 713, Schweser p. 322

Financial Statement Analysis: Applications

Projecting Performance

1. Forecast expected GDP growth
2. Forecast expected industry sales based on historical relationship with GDP
3. Consider expected change of firm's market share
4. Forecast expected firm sales
5. Use historical margins for stable firms (gross, operating, net) or individual forecast for each expense item
   - Remove non-recurring items
   - Historical margins are not relevant to new, volatile, or high fixed cost industries

© Kaplan, Inc.   22

LOS 33.b Forecast
CFAI p. 713, Schweser p. 322

Financial Statement Analysis: Applications

Forecasting Net Income and Cash Flow

1. Develop a spreadsheet based on the estimated growth rate of sales
2. Make assumptions about working capital, fixed assets, COGS, and SG&A as proportions of sales
3. Estimate interest rates for saving/borrowing, tax rate, and dividends
4. Project net income and cash flow based on assumptions

© Kaplan, Inc.   23

Financial Forecasting Example

- Sales expected to be $100 million in year 1 and increase 5% per year
- COGS = 20% of sales
- SG&A = 40% of sales
- Interest income = 5% of cash (beg. year)
- Tax rate = 30%   ▪ No dividends
- Non-cash working capital = 70% of sales (beginning non-cash working capital = $67 mil)
  - Fixed capital investment = 5% of sales

© Kaplan, Inc.

24

Financial Forecast

($ mil.)	Year 1	Year 2	Year 3
Sales	**100**	105	110
– COGS	20	21	22
– SG&A	40	42	44
+ Interest	0	1	2
Pretax income	40	43	46
– Taxes	12	13	14
Net income	28	30	32

© Kaplan, Inc.

25 - 4

Financial Forecast (continued)

($ mil.)	Beg.	Year 1	Year 2	Year 3
Working capital	67	70	73	77
Net income		28	30	32
– Inv. in working cap.		3	3	4
– Inv. in fixed capital		5	5	6
Change in cash		**20**	**22**	**22**
Beginning cash		0	20	42
Ending cash	**0**	**20**	**42**	**64**

© Kaplan, Inc.

26 - 6

Credit Risk

- Ability of issuer to meet interest and principal repayment on schedule (capacity)
  - Cash flow forecast focus
  - Variability of cash flows

Character
Capacity   ── 4 Cs
Collateral
Covenants   Also in Fixed Income

© Kaplan, Inc.

27

LOS 33.c Describe	Financial Statement
CFAI p. 723, Schweser p. 323	Analysis: Applications

Credit Scoring

Credit rating agencies employ formulas – weighted averages of several specific accounting ratios and business characteristics which include:

Scale and diversification: Size, product diversification, geographical diversification

Operational efficiency: Such items as operating ROA, operating margins, and EBITDA margins fall into this category, along with degree of vertical integration.

© Kaplan, Inc.

28

LOS 33.c Describe	Financial Statement
CFAI p. 723, Schweser p. 323	Analysis: Applications

Credit Scoring

Margin stability: Stability of profitability margins indicates a higher probability of repayment (leads to a better debt rating and a lower cost of debt capital).

Leverage: Coverage ratios of operating earnings, EBITDA, or some measure of free cash flow to interest expense or total debt make up the most important part of the credit rating formula.

© Kaplan, Inc.

29

LOS 33.d Describe	Financial Statement
CFAI p. 726, Schweser p. 324	Analysis: Applications

Equity Investment Screening

Screening: Applying a set of criteria to reduce a set of investments to a smaller subset with desired characteristics

Involves comparing ratios to min/max values

Growth investors: Focus on earnings growth

Value investors: Focus on low share price in relation to earnings or assets

Market oriented: Neither value or growth focused

© Kaplan, Inc.

30

LOS 33.e Explain	Financial Statement
CFAI p. 730, Schweser p. 324	Analysis: Applications

Analyst Adjustments

Adjust financial statements for **differences in accounting choices** (e.g., LIFO/FIFO, accelerated/straight line depreciation, revenue recognition criteria)

Adjust financial statements for **differences in accounting standards** (e.g., IFRS vs. U.S. GAAP)

© Kaplan, Inc.

31

LOS 33.e Explain
CFAI p. 730, Schweser p. 324

Financial Statement
Analysis: Applications

Analyst Adjustments

Required to ensure accounts are comparable before calculating ratios

Investments

- Held-to-maturity
- Available-for-sale
- Trading
- IFRS: available-for-sale exchange rate gains taken to income statement

© Kaplan, Inc.

32

LOS 33.e Explain
CFAI p. 730, Schweser p. 324

Financial Statement
Analysis: Applications

Analyst Adjustments

Inventory

FIFO/LIFO/AVCO

Property, plant, and equipment

- Depreciation methods
- Estimated lives
- Salvage values
- IFRS allows revaluation

Goodwill

- Internally generated—not capitalized
- Purchased—capitalized

© Kaplan, Inc.

33

LOS 33.e Explain
CFAI p. 730, Schweser p. 324

Financial Statement
Analysis: Applications

Analyst Adjustments

Off-balance-sheet finance

Finance leases versus operating leases

Equity accounted SPEs versus non-qualifying SPEs

Sale of accounts receivable

© Kaplan, Inc.

34

Financial Reporting and Analysis

Additional Problems

KAPLAN
UNIVERSITY
SCHOOL OF PROFESSIONAL
AND CONTINUING EDUCATION | SCHWESER

**CFA Curriculum Vol. 3,
R.32, Q.2, p. 697**

1) The information provided by a low-quality financial report will *most likely*:

A. decrease company value.

B. indicate earnings are not sustainable.

C. impede the assessment of earnings quality.

- 2

**Reference Level I CFA Curriculum,
Reading 33, Problem 10**

2)

$ millions	20X1	20X2
Gross fixed assets	2.8	2.8
Accum. depreciation	1.2	1.6

The average age and useful life of the company's fixed assets at the end of 20X2 are *closest* to:

- 5

Additional Problems

3) The action *least likely* to increase CFO in the current period is to:

A. reduce inventory.

B. capitalize the purchase cost of an asset.

C. report a finance lease as an operating lease.

- 2

**CFA Curriculum Vol. 3,
R.32, Q.10, p. 697**

4) Which of the following is *most likely* to reflect conservative accounting choices?

A. Decreased reported earnings in later periods.

B. Increased reported earnings in the current period.

C. Increased debt reported on the balance sheet at the end of the current period.

- 2

CFA Curriculum Vol. 3, R.32, Q.23, p. 699

5) Which of the following is an indication that a company may be recognizing revenue prematurely? Relative to its competitors, the company's:

A. asset turnover is decreasing.

B. receivables turnover is increasing.

C. days sales outstanding is increasing.

- 2

STUDY SESSION 9 ANSWERS

Additional Problems

1. C

2. Average age 4 years; average life 7 years

3. C

4. C

5. C

Notes

Notes

Notes

Notes

Notes

Notes

Notes